★

# AN ASSET BUILDER'S GUIDE TO

# YOUTH AND MONEY

A SEARCH INSTITUTE PUBLICATION

Search INSTITUTE

*Practical research benefiting children and youth*

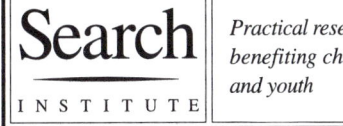

*An Asset Builder's Guide to Youth and Money* was developed with the generous support of Lilly Endowment as part of Habits of the Heart: Strengthening Traditions of Giving and Serving, an initiative of the Indiana Humanities Council.

**ABOUT SEARCH INSTITUTE**

Search Institute is an independent, nonprofit, nonsectarian organization whose mission is to advance the well-being of children and youth by generating knowledge and promoting its application. Search Institute conducts research and evaluation, develops publications and practical tools, and provides training and technical assistance. The institute collaborates with others to promote long-term organizational and cultural change that supports the healthy development of all children and adolescents. For a free information packet, call 800-888-7828.

**AN ASSET BUILDER'S GUIDE TO YOUTH AND MONEY**

Copyright © 1999 by Search Institute

All rights reserved. No part of this publication may be reproduced in any manner whatsoever, mechanical or electronic, without prior permission from the publisher except in brief quotations or summaries in articles or reviews, or as individual charts or graphs for educational use. For additional permission, write to Permissions at Search Institute.

700 South Third Street, Suite 210
Minneapolis, MN 55415
612-376-8955
800-888-7828
www.search-institute.org

10   9   8   7   6   5   4   3   2

ISBN: 1-57482-170-9

**CREDITS**

Author: Jolene L. Roehlkepartain
Editor: Jennifer Griffin-Wiesner
Design: Diane Gleba Hall
Production Coordinator: Jeannie Dressel

Cover: printed on recycled paper; 10% post-consumer waste.
Text: printed on recycled paper; 20% post-consumer waste.

*To my dad, Walter J. Roehlke, who taught me that the way you use money reveals what you value, what you believe in, and what you hope for.*

# CONTENTS

| | |
|---|---|
| **PREFACE** | vii |
| **INTRODUCTION** | 1 |
| **PART 1. THE ASSET APPROACH TO FINANCIAL RESPONSIBILITY** | 5 |
| What Do I Want to Know? | 6 |
| What Do I Want to Do? | 9 |
| Who Do I Want to Be? | 12 |
| **PART 2. CORE MONEY MANAGEMENT ISSUES** | 15 |
| **Financial Goals and Plans** | |
| Setting Financial Goals | 15 |
| Budgets | 19 |
| Banking | 22 |
| **Income** | |
| Earning | 25 |
| Being an Entrepreneur | 28 |
| **Saving** | |
| The Basics of Saving | 31 |
| Investing | 34 |
| **Giving** | |
| Introducing Giving | 38 |
| Charitable Giving | 41 |
| Giving to Religious Organizations | 44 |
| Giving Gifts | 47 |
| Fund-Raising | 50 |
| Youth Involvement in Grant Making | 53 |

**Spending**

| | |
|---|---|
| Your Spending Habits | 56 |
| Shopping | 59 |
| Using Credit Cards | 62 |
| Borrowing | 65 |
| Dealing with Debt | 68 |

## PART 3. WHAT OTHERS CAN DO TO MODEL AND TEACH FINANCIAL RESPONSIBILITY — 71

| | |
|---|---|
| How Families Can Model and Teach Financial Responsibility | 72 |
| How Schools Cans Model and Teach Financial Responsibility | 73 |
| How Youth-Serving Organizations Can Model and Teach Financial Responsibility | 74 |
| How Congregations Can Model and Teach Financial Responsibility | 75 |

## RECOMMENDED RESOURCES — 77

## GLOSSARY — 79

## NOTES — 83

# PREFACE

Habits of the Heart is an initiative of the Indiana Humanities Council that seeks to understand and nurture young people's habits of giving and serving in their communities. This book was developed by Search Institute as part of that project. Although much is known about youth and service, there is little in the way of research about or resources related to young people and philanthropic giving. As we talked with congregations, schools, and youth-serving organizations across the country (the types of organizations with the most frequent contact with and service to young people), it became clear that encouraging young people to give, and equipping them with the skills to do so wisely, is not common practice.

Helping young people be responsible stewards of resources is about much more than simply teaching them why and how to give. It's about helping them clarify their goals for their lives, what they want to learn, what experiences they hope to have, and what it means to them to be people of integrity. It's also about equipping them with the skills to manage money in ways that leave room for meeting basic needs, satisfying wants, *and* giving. With that foundation, issues of money and other resources can be addressed in ways that are meaningful, real, and make clear that planning, earning, saving, giving, and spending are all part of the larger picture of financial health and responsibility.

Young people have an incredible capacity for kindness, generosity, and personal and civic responsibility. They also have wants and needs that often come with price tags. This book seeks to provide tools for helping young people discover how financial management can move them beyond making choices based on what they want to have, and help them discover and act on what they want to know, do, and be.

# INTRODUCTION

When the author James Michener died in 1997, his estate was worth less than $10 million — a fortune to most, but a mere 8.5 percent of the total the author gave away during his 90 years. Michener could have given away a tiny fraction of his fortune and still have been remembered as a great philanthropist. He had, however, set a goal for himself of giving away at least 90 percent of his earnings, a goal he exceeded. Even after his death, his legacy of generosity carries on, as all royalties from his books are go to Swarthmore College, the school that in 1925 gave him a $2,000 scholarship. During his life he gave $7.2 million to Swarthmore, in addition to large sums to support authors with no income and no health insurance, to universities and museums, to a library, and to many other causes and organizations he cared about.[1]

By any standards, Michener was incredibly wealthy, but judging from what he did with that wealth, it would seem that how much he had was less important to him than what he did with it. Similarly, this book focuses not on how much young people have (or work toward having) but rather on helping them think about getting and using money in ways that are consistent with their values and priorities.

Outside of some economics classes and some family settings, there are few opportunities for young people to explore and study personal finances with the help of adults who care about them and are concerned about their well-being. If you ask adults who work with youth why this is so, they cite their own discomfort with financial matters, the belief that teaching about money is the responsibility of families, and a fear that the topic is difficult to deal with in groups of young people from disparate economic situations.

The irony is that most of us don't give a second thought to billboards, magazines, television, movies, and all of the other impersonal tools used to "teach" young people about how to use their money. By not dealing directly with money issues in places like schools, congregations, and youth-serving organizations — places that are focused on nurturing young people — we surrender this opportunity to those who are focused on selling to them.

To help young people make sound decisions about money matters, we can start by encouraging them to explore the answers to three questions:

- **What do I want to know?** What kinds of things do I want to learn in life? Do I want to continue my education after college? Are there things I can't or don't want to learn in a formal setting that I'd like to know more about (such as gardening or a second language)?
- **What do I want to do?** What experiences do I want to have now and in the future? Do I want to start my own business? Do I want to live simply? Do I want

to support organizations I care about? Do I want to travel? Do I want to go to the prom?

- **Who do I want to be?** What are my values and priorities? What really matters to me? What choices do I need to make to live in a way that is consistent with those values and priorities? What does it mean to have integrity?

By discovering the answers to these lifelong questions of identity and meaning, young people create for themselves filters through which to evaluate the many financial choices they face. Whether they struggle to meet basic needs, or can afford to buy more "things" than they know what to do with, all young people will be happier with their choices and feel better about having a sense of direction and purpose concerning their money issues.

Part 1 of this book focuses on helping young people explore the answers to these questions. It gives an overview of *development assets* — 40 factors that Search Institute researchers have found are closely related to overall positive development. It shows how these assets connect with and strengthen the development of financial skills and competencies. Part 2 is divided into five sections: financial goals and plans, income, saving, giving, and spending. We address 18 different money management topics within these categories. Finally, Part 3 highlights what congregations, youth-serving organizations, schools, and families can do to model and encourage financial responsibility.

You'll find brief introductions to each topic in Parts 1 and 2. These introductions are intended for adult readers, to provide background on each topic. However, they are written in a way that they could be used by young people as well. The glossary of terms at the end of the book can help clarify terms in these sections that may be unfamiliar. Following the introductions are questions for group discussion or personal reflection; ideas for group activities; examples of specific ways that assets connect with financial issues; interesting tips, quotes, or statistics related to the topic; and one or two reproducible worksheets. Part 3 includes reproducible handouts for families, schools, youth-serving organizations, and congregations.

## A Caution Before You Jump In

Because financial issues are deeply personal and can sometimes be difficult to deal with in public settings, we encourage you to read through this book with your own money management in mind before using it with young people. Ask yourself the same questions you will ask your youth. Try some of the same exercises you'll ask them to try. As you're doing these things, pay attention to your own biases and beliefs about financial matters. If you find there are difficult issues that arise repeatedly and are upsetting or frustrating for you, think about whether or not you need to attend to them personally before you can help young people do the same.

Those of us who are North Americans live in a society that is, in many ways, driven by acquiring and spending money. Collectively we control a large percentage of the world's resources, yet within our borders there is great economic disparity. There are also many different cultural and family norms about financial matters. Our hope is that this book provides you with information and tools that equip you to work within those contexts to encourage young people to find ways to live healthily, wisely, responsibly, and generously.

# SEARCH INSTITUTE'S 40 DEVELOPMENTAL ASSETS

Search Institute has identified the following building blocks of development that help young people grow up healthy, caring, and responsible.

## External Assets

### Support
**1. Family support**—Family life provides high levels of love and support.
**2. Positive family communication**—Young person and her or his parent(s) communicate positively, and young person is willing to seek advice and counsel from parents.
**3. Other adult relationships**—Young person receives support from three or more nonparent adults.
**4. Caring neighborhood**—Young person experiences caring neighbors.
**5. Caring school climate**—School provides a caring, encouraging environment.
**6. Parent involvement in schooling**—Parent(s) are actively involved in helping young person succeed in school.

### Empowerment
**7. Community values youth**—Young person perceives that adults in the community value youth.
**8. Youth as resources**—Young people are given useful roles in the community.
**9. Service to others**—Young person serves in the community one hour or more per week.
**10. Safety**—Young person feels safe at home, at school, and in the neighborhood.

### Boundaries and Expectations
**11. Family boundaries**—Family has clear rules and consequences and monitors the young person's whereabouts.
**12. School boundaries**—School provides clear rules and consequences.
**13. Neighborhood boundaries**—Neighbors take responsibility for monitoring young people's behavior.
**14. Adult role models**—Parent(s) and other adults model positive, responsible behavior.
**15. Positive peer influence**—Young person's best friends model responsible behavior.
**16. High expectations**—Both parent(s) and teachers encourage the young person to do well.

### Constructive Use of Time
**17. Creative activities**—Young person spends three or more hours per week in lessons or practice in music, theater, or other arts.
**18. Youth programs**—Young person spends three or more hours per week in sports, clubs, or organizations at school and/or in the community.
**19. Religious community**—Young person spends one or more hours per week in activities in a religious institution.
**20. Time at home**—Young person is out with friends "with nothing special to do" two or fewer nights per week.

## Internal Assets

### Commitment to Learning
**21. Achievement motivation**—Young person is motivated to do well in school.
**22. School engagement**—Young person is actively engaged in learning.
**23. Homework**—Young person reports doing at least one hour of homework every school day.
**24. Bonding to school**—Young person cares about her or his school.
**25. Reading for pleasure**—Young person reads for pleasure three or more hours per week.

### Positive Values
**26. Caring**—Young person places high value on helping other people.
**27. Equality and social justice**—Young person places high value on promoting equality and reducing hunger and poverty.
**28. Integrity**—Young person acts on convictions and stands up for her or his beliefs.
**29. Honesty**—Young person "tells the truth even when it is not easy."
**30. Responsibility**—Young person accepts and takes personal responsibility.
**31. Restraint**—Young person believes it is important not to be sexually active or to use alcohol or other drugs.

### Social Competencies
**32. Planning and decision making**—Young person knows how to plan ahead and make choices.
**33. Interpersonal competence**—Young person has empathy, sensitivity, and friendship skills.
**34. Cultural competence**—Young person has knowledge of and comfort with people of different cultural/racial/ethnic backgrounds.
**35. Resistance skills**—Young person can resist negative peer pressure and dangerous situations.
**36. Peaceful conflict resolution**—Young person seeks to resolve conflict nonviolently.

### Positive Identity
**37. Personal power**—Young person feels he or she has control over "things that happen to me."
**38. Self-esteem**—Young person reports having a high self-esteem.
**39. Sense of purpose**—Young person reports that "my life has a purpose."
**40. Positive view of personal future**—Young person is optimistic about her or his personal future.

This page may be reproduced for educational, noncommercial uses only. Copyright © 1997 by Search Institute, 700 South Third Street, Suite 210, Minneapolis, MN 55415; 800-888-7828; www.search-institute.org.

# 40 ELEMENTOS FUNDAMENTALES DEL DESARROLLO

La investigación realizada por el Instituto Search ha identificado los siguientes elementos fundamentales del desarrollo como instrumentos para ayudar a los jóvenes a crecer sanos, interesados en el bienestar común y a ser responsables.

## Apoyo

**1. Apoyo familiar**—La vida familiar brinda altos niveles de amor y apoyo.
**2. Comunicación familiar positiva**—El (La) joven y sus padres se comunican positivamente. Los jóvenes están dispuestos a buscar consejo y consuelo en sus padres.
**3. Otras relaciones con adultos**—Además de sus padres, los jóvenes reciben apoyo de tres o más personas adultas que no son sus parientes.
**4. Una comunidad comprometida**—El (La) joven experimenta el interés de sus vecinos por su bienestar.
**5. Un plantel educativo que se interesa por el (la) joven**—La escuela proporciona un ambiente que anima y se preocupa por la juventud.
**6. La participación de los padres en las actividades escolares**—Los padres participan activamente ayudando a los jóvenes a tener éxito en la escuela.

## Fortalecimiento

**7. La comunidad valora a la juventud**—El (La) joven percibe que los adultos en la comunidad valoran a la juventud.
**8. La juventud como un recurso**—Se le brinda a los jóvenes la oportunidad de tomar un papel útil en la comunidad.
**9. Servicio a los demás**—La gente joven participa brindando servicios a su comunidad una hora o más a la semana.
**10. Seguridad**—Los jóvenes se sienten seguros en casa, en la escuela y en el vecindario.

## Límites y expectativas

**11. Límites familiares**—La familia tiene reglas y consecuencias bien claras, además vigila las actividades de los jóvenes.
**12. Límites escolares**—En la escuela proporciona reglas y consecuencias bien claras.
**13. Límites vecinales**—Los vecinos asumen la responsabilidad de vigilar el comportamiento de los jóvenes.
**14. El comportamiento de los adultos como ejemplo**—Los padres y otros adultos tienen un comportamiento positivo y responsable.
**15. Compañeros como influencia positiva**—Los mejores amigos del (la) joven son un buen ejemplo de comportamiento responsable.
**16. Altas expectativas**—Ambos padres y maestros motivan a los jóvenes para que tengan éxito.

## Uso constructivo del tiempo

**17. Actividades creativas**—Los jóvenes pasan tres horas o más a la semana en lecciones de música, teatro u otras artes.
**18. Programas juveniles**—Los jóvenes pasan tres horas o más a la semana practicando algún deporte, o en organizaciones en la escuela o de la comunidad.
**19. Comunidad religiosa**—Los jóvenes pasan una hora o más a la semana en actividades organizadas por alguna institución religiosa.
**20. Tiempo en casa**—Los jóvenes conviven con sus amigos "sin nada especial que hacer" dos o pocas noches por semana.

## Compromiso con el aprendizaje

**21. Motivación por sus logros**—El (La) joven es motivado(a) para que salga bien en la escuela.
**22. Compromiso con la escuela**—El (La) joven participa activamente con el aprendizaje.
**23. Tarea**—El (La) joven debe hacer su tarea escolar por lo menos durante una hora cada día de clases.
**24. Preocuparse por la escuela**—Al (A la) joven debe importarle su escuela.
**25. Leer por placer**—El (La) joven lee por placer tres horas o más por semana.

Valores positivos

**26. Preocuparse por los demás**—El (La) joven valora ayudar a los demás.
**27. Igualdad y justicia social**—Para el (la) joven tiene mucho valor el promover la igualdad y reducir el hambre y la pobreza.
**28. Integridad**—El (La) joven actúa con convicción y defiende sus creencias.
**29. Honestidad**—El (La) joven "dice la verdad aún cuando esto no sea fácil".
**30. Responsabilidad**—El (La) joven acepta y toma responsabilidad por su persona.
**31. Abstinencia**—El (La) joven cree que es importante no estar activo(a) sexualmente, ni usar alcohol u otras drogas.

## Capacidad social

**32. Planeación y toma de decisiones**—El (La) joven sabe cómo planear y hacer elecciones.
**33. Capacidad interpersonal**—El (La) joven es sympático, sensible y hábil para hacer amistades.
**34. Capacidad cultural**—El (La) joven tiene conocimiento de y sabe convivir con gente de diferente marco cultural, racial o étnico.
**35. Habilidad de resistencia**—El (La) joven puede resistir la presión negativa de los compañeros así como las situaciones peligrosas.
**36. Solución pacífica de conflictos**—El (La) joven busca resolver los conflictos sin violencia.

## Identidad positiva

**37. Poder personal**—El (La) joven siente que él o ella tiene el control de "las cosas que le suceden".
**38. Auto-estima**—El (La) joven afirma tener una alta auto-estima.
**39. Sentido de propósito**—El (La) joven afirma que "mi vida tiene un propósito".
**40. Visión positiva del futuro personal**—El (La) joven es optimista sobre su futuro mismo.

El permiso para reproducir este manual es otorgado con propósitos educativos, no comerciales. Derechos reservados @ 1998 por Search Institute, 700 South Third Street, Minneapolis, MN 55415, 800-888-7828; www.search-institute.org.

# PART 1
# THE ASSET APPROACH
# TO FINANCIAL RESPONSIBILITY

For more than 30 years, researchers at Search Institute have been studying healthy youth development. Since the late 1980s much of that work has focused on developmental assets—the opportunities, skills, relationships, values, and self-perceptions that help young people thrive. They have identified 40 of these assets, 20 internal and 20 external (see page 3). External assets are the opportunities and relationships that others provide for or develop with young people. Internal assets are the values, beliefs, and commitments that grow within young people that guide them on the paths they choose and the way they interact with others and the world.

The more assets young people have, the more likely they are to do things that are good for themselves and others, such as succeed in school, volunteer in their communities, and take on leadership roles. These assets also have a positive impact on health-compromising behaviors such as being violent, using alcohol and other drugs, and committing crimes. As young people's experiences of assets increase, their rates of involvement in these and similar behaviors decrease.

The relationship between assets and the choices youth make has several implications related to money. One is that young people who have more assets report making more sound choices related to money. They are less likely than other teens to gamble, and they are more likely to "save money for something special rather than spend it all right away." A second, less direct, but equally important, relationship is between assets and behaviors such as gambling, and alcohol, tobacco, and other drug use, all of which can be tremendously expensive habits. These and other types of health-compromising behaviors decrease as young people's experiences of assets increase. Third, asset-rich young people are better equipped to answer the question "What do I want to know, do, and be?" because they have role models to emulate, positive roles and relationships in their families and communities, plans and hopes for the future, a commitment to learning, clarity about their personal values, and skills and competencies for acting on those values. Perhaps the most important part of an asset approach to teaching young people about finances is that the focus is on the person first and money second. While this may seem like a simple concept, it is counter to many of our society's accepted attitudes and beliefs about money. The sidebar on the next page shows some of the differences.

## SOME STEREOTYPICAL AMERICAN ATTITUDES ABOUT MONEY

▶ Financial independence comes from pulling yourself up by your own bootstraps.
▶ The rich get richer, and the poor get poorer.
▶ To be successful, work more and work harder to earn money.
▶ Only people with a lot of money can afford to give.
▶ Money buys happiness.
▶ More is better.
▶ Saving money makes us secure.
▶ We grow when we become upwardly mobile.
▶ How much money you have is what's important.

## ASSET-BUILDING ATTITUDES ABOUT MONEY

▶ We are interdependent, and there are responsible ways to seek support.
▶ Everyone can become psychologically rich and empowered through learning financial skills and identifying personal values and priorities.
▶ Success is knowing what you want to know, doing what you want to do, and being who you want to be and having financial goals that are consistent with those things.
▶ It's an asset to value caring (asset #26) and to serve others (asset #9). Everyone can afford to give their time, talents, or money in some way.
▶ Happiness comes from recognizing, enjoying, and appreciating what we have; having high expectations for a positive personal future; and taking responsibility for achieving those goals.
▶ Everything has limits and boundaries—including the benefits of money.
▶ Developing our personal identity and having close relationships make us secure. Saving money is a way to achieve our dreams and plan our future.
▶ Valuing upward mobility often comes at the cost of building asset #27 (equality and social justice). Developing our personal identities is how we grow.
▶ How you get money and what you choose to do with it are more important than what you have.

Keeping these differences in mind when working on money issues with young people can assist you in helping them focus on the things that really matter to them. We recommend that before you launch into money management issues, you use the ideas and activities that follow to help youth begin to answer the questions of what they want to know, do, and be.

## What Do I Want to Know?

Learning transcends schools, congregations, cocurricular activities, and other formal settings for developing skills and gathering information. We learn things every day in the interactions we have with people, the places we visit, the "work" we do (whether it's at home, school, in an office, or elsewhere), and the things we do for fun or relaxation.

Learning things because they happen and being intentional about having experiences that teach us are very different. Setting goals for what and how you want to learn can set you on a course for lifelong learning with a focus and purpose.

Once you have a sense of the things you want to know and the learning paths you want to take, you can begin to figure out related costs and creative ways of reducing and/or covering those costs. You also have a basis for making choices for how to use money. For example, if you know you want to continue your formal education beyond high school, you can look into the cost of different institutions, the possibilities for scholarships and work study, and changes you might have to make in your spending or earning in order to afford the education you want. If you know you want to learn another language by traveling abroad, you can research programs that combine work and travel, or what it takes to get a work visa for another country.

Clearly, people's goals and interests evolve over their lifetimes. Unfortunately, many people don't have good skills for recognizing or knowing how to

## Part 1: The Asset Approach to Financial Responsibility

act on those goals and interests. Developing these skills can empower you to take charge of your life, give you a sense of purpose, and motivate you to work toward financial health.

### Think about It

- What are your short-term (one or two years) goals for learning? How do these goals fit with your short-term financial goals?
- What things would you like to learn in your lifetime?
- Do your learning goals for your life involve needing money for formal training, traveling, buying equipment, or other costs?
- If your learning goals require money, are you doing things to earn and save money now so that you can achieve your goals later? What kinds of things are you doing?

###  Try It

- Visit a career or workforce development center that is accustomed to dealing with young people. Arrange for your group to have a tour of the center and learn what services are available to them as they think about what kinds of jobs and careers they might like to pursue. Talk with them about how the best jobs are those that combine people's interests with their skills. Discuss the potential downsides to pursuing a career based primarily on how much money you want to make.
- Give each young person an index card. Ask them to write down three interests they have that they don't think they will learn about in middle or high school. If they're not sure what you mean, give them examples such as aerobics, gourmet cooking, or fly-fishing. Ask them to talk about each of these interests with at least one adult in the next month and to get ideas from the adult about how they might learn more about these interests.
- Encourage them to look into the costs associated and ways to keep those costs down.

### Asset Connections

- Five of the assets are in the commitment-to-learning category. Helping young people identify their learning and knowledge goals can enhance their achievement motivation (#21), school engagement (#22), time spent on homework (#23), and reading for pleasure (#25). Experiencing these assets may help them see that there are many affordable ways to learn.
- Having a clear sense of the kinds of things they want to know and learn about can add to young people's sense of purpose in life (asset #39). Having a sense of purpose can influence all aspects of personal finances.

### Did You Know?

Finding and financing (if necessary) nonschool learning alternatives may be more important than people realize, since only about one-quarter (26 percent) of young people surveyed by Public Agenda say they get excited by something they study in school every day or almost every day.[2]

### Earning Money and Learning Can Go Hand in Hand

Most young people say that learning is an important part of why they work for pay. Eighty-four percent of teenagers surveyed by researchers at the University of Michigan say that getting a job in which they learn new things and acquire new skills is very or pretty important.[3]

## WRITE ABOUT IT

## WHAT I WANT TO LEARN

Scattered on the page below (in no particular order), write as many things as you can think of that you would like to learn more about. Think about regular school subjects such as math and writing, as well as other things like scuba diving, knitting, or woodworking. You can write 5 things or 50 or more.

A big part of learning about something is just taking the initiative to sign up for a class, get a book on the subject, or talk to someone who knows about it. Once you've written down all of your ideas, circle the one that you want to work on first. If you are not sure how you might start learning about that topic, ask a friend, a teacher, your parent or guardian, or someone else who might have an idea. Keep asking different people until you find someone who can and will help you. More important, don't let finances get in your way. For example, community education classes are often very inexpensive, and other organizations have sliding fee scales (you pay what you can afford).

## What Do I Want to Do?

Like learning and knowing things, it's pretty easy to just coast along and do whatever you feel like doing at the moment or whatever the people around you are doing. But whether you put a lot of thought into things or just let them happen, your actions reflect what you care about and what is important to you. Your actions also have an impact on the world around you—individuals, your neighborhood, an organization, your community, and even the world.

Taking time to think about the things you really hope to do in your life can help you make choices and set you on a course to accomplish what you intend to do. This can range from working for human rights to being a writer to playing professional basketball to taking care of your family.

Of course, doing things often costs money, either directly or indirectly. For example, if you plan to work for human rights by volunteering a lot of your time, you'll need to find ways to meet your basic needs for food and shelter. If being a writer means working on a novel, you'll have to figure out how to support yourself until you get your first well-paying book deal. If taking care of your family means paying for someone's college education or hiring a nurse to care for a person who becomes ill, you'll need to have the financial reserves to do that.

Understanding the connections between your choices about money and your personal goals can help you do the things you really want to in life.

 **Think about It**

- Do you think that what you do with your money is a reflection of your values? Why or why not?
- Is it important to do things with your money that help other people (such as give to charity or support causes such as human rights)? Why or why not?
- Are there people whom you admire because of what they do with their money? What kinds of things do they do?
- What are the top three things you want to do in the next year? five years? in your lifetime? Do you need money to be able to do those things?

 **Try It**

- Ask young people to write "personals" ads about themselves that highlight the things they do. This may include school, cocurricular activities, hobbies, service and volunteering, and other activities. After they have written their ads, ask them to talk about how they feel about what they wrote. Were they happy with the things they were able to write about themselves? Are there things they would like to do, but don't? Do they do too much? too little? Are there things they currently do that they don't want to do anymore? How many of their activities involve making or spending money? Does money influence what they choose to do?
- Ask each young person to identify one adult who has done something that the young person thinks is really unique, interesting, exciting, scary, or all of these. Encourage the young people to interview the adult, asking questions about the thing the adult did, if it cost money, if the adult planned it or it just happened, how the adult feels about it now, if it was worth the cost, and whether or not he or she would do it again. As a group, brainstorm a list of questions before the interviews so that young people have ideas about what to ask.

**Asset Connections**

- Being clear about what they want to do in their lives can help young people understand that they have control over things that happen to them (asset #37: personal power).
- Helping young people see that there are many

things they can do to make a difference in their neighborhoods, communities, or beyond builds asset #8 (youth as resources).

### ❓ Did You Know?

Can you imagine what you would do with $44 million? In Dubai, a state of the United Arab Emirates, the 1981 wedding of the princess and the son of a sheik lasted seven days and cost that much, landing it a spot in *The Guinness Book of World Records* as the most expensive wedding ever.[4]

### 💲 You Can Use Money to Make a Difference

"Money is a powerful tool to create change, not only in your life, but also in our country and our world."

—Ruth Hayden, author of *How to Turn Your Money Life Around*[5]

Part 1: The Asset Approach to Financial Responsibility

**WRITE ABOUT IT**

## BELIEVING IN A POSITIVE FUTURE

In *The Color of Water,* author James McBride writes of growing up in poverty in the Brooklyn Red Hook projects as 1 of 12 children of a very determined woman. Ruth McBride Jordan, James's mother, put all of her children and herself through college.

The McBride children are now the director of a city health department, a psychologist, a medical doctor, the chair of a department at a university, a chemistry researcher, an office manager for a medical practice, a computer consultant, teachers (3), a writer and composer, and a student. All are highly successful and making important contributions to their communities. Jordan received a degree in social work administration at the age of 65.

Despite a very challenging financial situation—poverty, two husbands who died, leaving her as the sole provider for a very large family—Jordan was determined to stay focused on a positive future for herself and her family. Her story shows us that we can do things that seem impossible, if we want to badly enough.

**What are your hopes for your future?** _____

_____
_____
_____
_____
_____
_____
_____
_____
_____
_____

**Are there financial barriers that you think might keep you from reaching your dreams?** _____

_____
_____
_____
_____
_____
_____
_____
_____
_____
_____

Stories like Ruth McBride Jordan's are inspiring and not as rare as we might think. There are probably people close to you who have lived they way they wanted to, despite financial odds. Ask others (such as parents, guardians, grandparents, other relatives, teachers, youth workers, coaches, neighbors, friends) about their experiences doing things they never thought they would have enough money to do. How did they do it? Was it hard? What can you learn from their experiences?

## Who Do I Want to Be?

What kind of a person am I? How do others perceive me? Am I valued and valuable? Loving and lovable? Am I normal? These are all questions that most people ask themselves throughout their lives, and with special intensity during adolescence. As young people seek to claim their own individuality and figure out how they fit in the world, they can feel pride, excitement, confidence, frustration, confusion, anger, and even shame.

"Going public" with this exploration by talking and thinking about it with others can bring a needed sense of normalcy and acceptance of this process. Being is different from knowing and doing, although none of these can be separated from the others. Being is unique in that it is more internally focused than doing, and more personal than knowing. It includes identifying your values and figuring out how to live in ways that are true to those values, and thus being a person of integrity. It may be the most difficult of the three areas to explore with others, because the answers are often unclear and evolving, and the implications can be less apparent. The money implications, too, may be less evident because knowing and doing can involve very concrete actions, whereas being is more about how one is in the world. But, even if you only approach the subject and don't go into it with much depth, you will have affirmed that it is an important question and one worth asking.

### Think about It

- What does the word integrity mean to you? Do you know people who you think have integrity? What are they like?
- What are your values and priorities? What's important to you? What do you really care about?
- How have you seen other people reveal their values and priorities by the way they live?
- Do you think there are connections between becoming the person you want to be and how you handle money matters? Why or why not?

###  Try It

- Bring in some newspapers and magazines that have articles about how people have used their money (such as buying or starting companies, making a contribution to an organization or cause, or buying a notable item). Clip the articles and pass them around for everyone to glance at or read. As a group, discuss what you think the values and priorities are of the person or people featured based on how they used their money. Then have young people write news stories they would like to have written about themselves in the future regarding how their use of money reflects their values and priorities.
- On a large sheet of paper or a chalkboard draw two columns. Label one Positive Examples and the other Negative Examples. As a group, name people outside of the group who live in ways that reflect positive values and priorities (encourage young people to name examples from their personal experience, their observations of people around them, and what they hear, see, and read in the media). List the names in the positive examples column. Then ask for negative examples and list these.

### Asset Connections

- Helping young people identify what kinds of people they want to be includes exploring the positive values (assets #26–31) that are important to them.
- Young people who have a clear sense of who they want to be probably have asset #40 (positive view of personal future).

## Did You Know?

More young people care about being wealthy than about making a contribution to society. Twenty-five percent of teenagers in one national study said that having lots of money is extremely important to them, while 20 percent said the same things about making a contribution to society.[6]

## Your Value Has Nothing to Do with Money

"Understanding what money does is the first step in understanding what it doesn't do—the first step [is] . . . not to confuse self-worth with net worth."

—Neal S. Godfrey, author of *A Penny Saved*[7]

## WRITE ABOUT IT

# MONEY AND YOUR VALUES

Having integrity means living in a way that is consistent with your values, beliefs, and priorities. How you get and use money is an important part of that. In the following chart list five of your values (such as being honest or caring for others). Then give examples of how you can act on those values through your earning, saving, giving, and spending. See the example to get you started.

**Value**

*I care about animals and animal rights.*

**Earning**

*Work for an organization such as a humane society that cares for animals in need.*

**Saving**

*Save money so I can adopt a pet from an animal shelter.*

**Giving**

*Donate money to an organization that works toward preserving natural habitat.*

**Spending**

*I will not buy clothing or accessories made from animals.*

Acting on personal values isn't always easy, and a little support from others can help a lot. You can support others by noticing and commenting when they do things with integrity. When you make choices based on your values, tell someone else about it.

# PART 2
# CORE MONEY MANAGEMENT ISSUES

## Financial Goals and Plans

The first step toward financial health is understanding the basics of managing money. That means knowing how to plan for the future in ways that integrate life goals and money matters, developing a budget that is realistic and balanced, and working with the institutions and organizations that provide financial services.

### Setting Financial Goals

A good place to start when trying to set personal financial goals is to think about the other goals you have in life such as post–high school education, starting a business, traveling, buying something big like a car or house, or having a family. All of these goals — and many others — require some sort of funding. Some people also have goals related to making a difference for others through such things as volunteering, supporting organizations dedicated to protecting the environment, working toward social justice, or helping friends or family become economically self-sufficient. These too can have direct and indirect costs that will need to be covered. Being clear about these personal goals can set the stage for establishing financial goals that can help you achieve your dreams.

When setting financial goals, think about all the areas of your life and what goals you have related to what you want to know, what you want to do, and who you want to be. If you have a hard time thinking beyond next week or month, imagine what you want your life to be like in 5 or 10 years, including where you will live, if you will have a job, the kinds of activities you will be involved in, and the causes or organizations you will support.

 **Think about It**

- Have you ever set personal goals for yourself?
- Was it helpful for you to have set those goals? Why or why not?
- What are some of your current personal goals?
- What money or other resources do you need to achieve your personal goals?
- Have you thought about how you might get that money or those resources?
- Have you ever set financial goals? Why or why not?
- Do you think that having financial goals is an important step in achieving your personal goals? Why or why not?
- Do you know anyone who sets financial goals who might be able to help you set yours?

## Try It

- Give young people paper and a pen or pencil. Ask them to draw three columns and label them Immediate Personal Goals (0–1 year), Short-Term Personal Goals (2–4 years), and Long-Term Personal Goals (5 or more years). Ask them to list two to three goals in each column. When they finish, hand out copies of My Financial Goals (page 18) and ask them to complete it. When they finish, talk as a group about the connections between personal and financial goals.

- Place a 12-foot piece of masking tape on the floor. Explain that the tape represents a continuum, meaning that the ends are opposite extremes. Tell them that you are going to call out statements about financial goals and two extreme views related to those statements. Use statements such as, Setting financial goals is simple or complex; Setting financial goals is important or not important; Setting financial goals is time consuming or not time consuming; Setting financial goals is difficult or easy; I have a lot of or no experience setting financial goals. After each statement tell them which end of the continuum represents which extreme and ask them to go to a spot that best reflects their views. They do not need to go to one end or the other. After everyone has found a place on the continuum, ask for a few people to explain why they chose the spot they did. At the end of the exercise, discuss questions such as, Do you have strong feelings about setting financial goals? Are they mostly positive or negative? Why do you think you have the attitude you have about financial goals? Has your attitude changed? If so, why?

- Give young people a personal financial survey. Ask them to write down the answers to a series of questions with yes or no answers. Ask questions such as, Do you have financial goals for yourself? Do you have a budget? Do you track your expenses and income? Do you have a place where you store financial records? Do you have an adult to talk to about financial matters? Do you feel good about how you handle your finances? After they've completed the survey ask them to tally their yes responses. Explain that the yes responses represent power they have over their personal finances. Encourage them to work toward more yes responses. If you like, you could give young people the survey again after leading them through some of the activities in this book.

- Invite someone who sets personal financial goals to talk to your group about her or his experiences. It doesn't have to be someone who works in financial planning, but it should be someone who takes goal setting seriously. In preparation for the speaker, brainstorm with young people some questions to ask. Ask the speaker to talk about the difference having financial goals has made in her or his life and then have time for young people to ask questions.

## Asset Connections

- Setting financial goals and making decisions about money based on those goals is all about asset #32 (planning and decision making).
- Having financial goals can give young people a strong sense of asset #37 (personal power).
- Young people who have financial goals focused on giving to people, organizations, and causes probably experience at least two assets: youth as resources (#8) and equality and social justice (#27).

## Did You Know?

Research reveals that people who make financial plans are much more confident than nonplanners that they have made the right financial choices.[8]

## You're the Expert

"Few people need to [hire a professional] financial planner," according to *The Complete Guide to Managing Your Money*. "Setting goals, revising them as needed, and investing assets according to sound principles is safer and more sensible."[9]

Part 2: Core Money Management Issues

**WRITE ABOUT IT**

# MY FINANCIAL GOALS

Think about your immediate, short-term, and long-term financial goals. Use this chart to identify them and then store this chart in a safe place. Once a year (maybe on New Year's or on April 15—tax day) take out the chart and see how you've done. Then update the chart to reflect any changes.

| Time Frame for Financial Goals | Sample Goals | Your Goals |
|---|---|---|
| **Immediate** (present to 1 year) | ▶ Start saving 1% of my income from jobs, gifts, and other sources<br>▶ Start giving 1% of my income to charity<br>▶ Open a savings account | |
| **Short-term** (2 to 4 years) | ▶ Increase by 1% each year the portion of my income that I save<br>▶ Increase by 1% each year the portion of my income that I give to charity<br>▶ Get a regular part-time job<br>▶ Open a checking account<br>▶ Save enough to buy a stereo | |
| **Long-term** (5 years or more) | ▶ Increase by 1% each year the portion of my income that I save until I reach 10%<br>▶ Increase by 1% each year the portion of my income that I give to charity until I reach 10%<br>▶ Save $2,000 for my education after high school | |

It can be difficult to create and work toward realistic, yet challenging financial goals, particularly at first. The important thing is to start somewhere and keep adjusting until you get to a point where you are making progress without feeling like your goals are a burden or unattainable. To help keep you on track, think of ways to celebrate small successes such as taking the first step of creating a financial plan. Then how can you keep motivated to work toward and update it on a regular basis?

This page may be reproduced for educational, noncommercial uses only. From *An Asset Builder's Guide to Youth and Money* by Jolene L. Roehlkepartain. Copyright © 1999 by Search Institute, 700 South Third Street, Suite 210, Minneapolis, MN 55415; 800-888-7828; www.search-institute.org.

## Budgets

The basic purpose of having a budget and sticking to it is to make sure that you are not paying out more than you are bringing in. That's easier said than done for some people, but it is the key to financial health because while money can't buy happiness, not having enough money can lead to a lot of stress, frustration, and unhappiness.

For most people the process of budgeting is fairly straightforward but not terribly fun. It requires keeping track of every income source and every expenditure, probably for several months. Keeping track of all income and output means paying *a lot of* attention to details. In the beginning, it can feel like the budget has become the central focus of your life. But it's important to stick with it for a while because you will probably begin to notice patterns that you didn't know you had (such as buying ice cream twice a week or spending a lot of money on gifts for friends). And even once you've set up a budget that seems to make sense, you'll find that things change or that your expectations were unrealistic. Once you are aware of these issues you can probably make adjustments in your budget or in your habits in order to accommodate them.

Lots of things can happen when people start the budgeting process. Some are appalled by how much money they spend. Others are pleased to find that they live well within their means without making any special effort. And others find or confirm what they already knew: that they simply aren't bringing in enough money to cover all of their expenses. In these cases, budgets can help us understand why we can't get ahead, and what some possibilities are for limiting expenses or increasing income.

Having a budget won't solve all financial problems, but as financial expert Jonathan Pond points out, it can highlight the roots of those problems and identify possible ways of dealing with them.[10]

 **Think about It**

- Do you have a clear sense of your income and your expenses? Why or why not?
- Do you currently follow a budget? Why or why not?
- Have you ever carefully tracked your income and expenses? Was it helpful? Why or why not?
- Does anyone in your family follow a budget? If you're not sure, ask them.
- Do you think having a budget is a good idea? Why or why not?
- Are you motivated to have a budget? If so, what's motivating you?
- What things keep you from starting or updating a budget?

 **Try It**

- On a large piece of paper draw two columns, one labeled "Pros" (the good things) and the other labeled "Cons" (the bad things). As a group, brainstorm a list of the pros and cons of the process of developing and sticking to a budget. When you finish creating the lists, compare the length, the relative importance of the items on each, and positive ways to deal with the cons.
- On a chalkboard or large piece of paper draw two columns and label each with a name (don't use the names of anyone in your group). In the first column list the following: paper route +$3, candy bar –55¢, soft drink –75¢, allowance +$5, gift from grandparent +$5, and music CD –$12. In the second column list baby-sitting +$20, movie –$7, popcorn at movie –$2, magazine -$3, gift from uncle +$5, pack of gum –60¢, giving away –10% of income, and saving –10% of income. Then ask each person to total the income and expenses for the two people and compare their overall financial health. Afterward ask young people if they were surprised by the differences they found. Talk about how tracking this level of detail can be

tedious but is important to developing an accurate budget. Also point out that simply listing income and expenses isn't enough to get an accurate financial picture and that doing the calculations is important.

- Ask those young people who keep a written budget and are willing to share their method to bring copies (without any figures included) to share with the rest of the group. Point out that different people have different needs from budgets and encourage youth to use the samples from their peers as starting points for creating a new budget or improving the one they have.

## Asset Connections

- Having the skills to create and follow a budget can help young people reach their goals and thus build asset #37 (personal power).

- Successful budgeting builds asset #32 (planning and decision making). An up-to-date budget is the beginning of a financial plan that can lead to making sound decisions about money.

## Did You Know?

The top three reasons budgets fail are:
- Lack of commitment;
- Unrealistic goals; and
- A serious emergency such as illness or sudden unemployment.[11]

**WRITE ABOUT IT**

# A BUDGET STARTER

Although your ideal budget is the one that you create based on your needs and wants, you can use this budget to get started.

**Monthly Income**

$ _____ Allowance

$ _____ Gifts

$ _____ Part-time job

$ _____ Other

$ _____ **Total Monthly Income**

$ _____ Giving goal  ( _____ %)

$ _____ Saving goal  ( _____ %)

$ _____ **NET SPENDABLE INCOME** (total income minus the amount of your giving and saving)

**Monthly Expenses**

$ _____ Transportation (mass transit passes and tokens, cab fare, car insurance, gas, car maintenance, car repairs, car license, car payments)

$ _____ Household contributions (groceries, rent, utilities)

$ _____ Clothing (clothes, shoes, accessories)

$ _____ Entertainment (arcade games, movies, video rentals, concerts, dances, sporting events)

$ _____ Special purchases (cosmetics, toiletries, haircuts or styling, music CDs, videos, gifts for friends or family, Internet bill, pager bill, magazines, books, comic books)

$ _____ Food (eating out, snacks, school lunch)

$ _____ Other

$ _____ **Total Monthly Expenses**

Add up your expenses. This total should be equal to or less than the net spendable income near the top of the budget sheet. How much does your actual budget reflect your priorities and plans? Do you have flexibility in cases of emergency or special occasions? Could you save or give away even more than you do already? Are there adjustments you can make in how you use your money that will better reflect what you want to know, do, and be?

This page may be reproduced for educational, noncommercial uses only. From *An Asset Builder's Guide to Youth and Money* by Jolene L. Roehlkepartain. Copyright © 1999 by Search Institute, 700 South Third Street, Suite 210, Minneapolis, MN 55415; 800-888-7828; www.search-institute.org.

## Banking

The days of kids saving money by keeping coins in a piggy bank or jar may very well be over. There is a growing trend toward banking options that are aimed specifically at young people. In Denver, for example, the Young American's Bank offers services that include savings, checking, and loans to people under 22. Within a year of opening in 1987, 3,100 young people had started accounts with the bank, 75 percent of them being savings accounts with an average balance of $150 and an average customer age of 9. The average checking customer is 14 and has a balance of $250. Loans are made to cover cars, bicycles, clothes, and other purchases. According to Young American's president, Linda Sanders, one young man even took out a loan to buy a dog.[12]

In addition to for-profit banks — organizations designed to make money for their owners and/or shareholders — there are cooperative groups known as credit unions, which offer many of the same services as banks. These are nonprofit organizations in which members' money is pooled to make loans at reasonable rates and investments that yield returns on savings. Credit union members usually share something in common such as a profession or the community in which they live or work. Millions of people choose to bank with credit unions.

While banking with an institution can have its rewards (such as interest earnings and protection against loss or theft), it's important to make informed decisions about which services you will use, and to be knowledgeable enough to follow what is happening with your money. Banks and credit unions can and do make mistakes. There are also fees associated with many of the services offered. Evaluating the pros and cons of different options and knowing how to look for errors are important skills, whether you want a basic savings account or a complex set of services.

 **Think about It**

- What do you currently know about banking? What would you like to learn?
- How do you feel when you walk into a bank or credit union? Do you like this feeling? Why or why not?
- Would you be comfortable saving your money through a bank or credit union? Why or why not?
- Do you think it's important to look over your statement each month and make sure it is consistent with your own records? Why or why not? If you have an account, is this something you do?
- What kinds of banking services do you think you'll want or need in the future? Do you think it's important to start learning about those things now?

 **Try It**

- As a group, brainstorm a list of banking services young people think they are most likely to use now and in the future. The things they list might include automated teller machines (ATMs), checking and savings accounts, loans, and banking by phone or email. Then have them research the costs of these services (urge them to look for the hidden costs as well as obvious ones). Encourage them to look for things like differences in charges depending on minimum balance. You can ask young people to work alone or in groups. Either way, be sure they gather information from several different banks or credit unions so that they can make comparisons. After they have gathered the information, ask young people to share it with the group. Consider creating a comparison chart and giving a copy to each young person.
- Brainstorm a list of questions young people have about banking. Arrange to visit a bank or credit union in your community and talk with a staff person about the questions. Ask for a tour and for written material that young people can take home.

- Ask each young person in your group to create a mock checkbook and checks (make a sample so that they have a model). Show them how to write checks and talk about the importance of keeping track of each one. Point out that checks are different from credit cards in that once you run out of money in your account, you can't write any more checks, even if you still have blanks in your book. Then role-play situations such as making a deposit, writing checks for food, rent, and other expenses, and making tax-deductible donations. You can make the role-playing as simple or as complex as you like. It can be a one-time activity or an ongoing exercise. To make it seem more real, offer a range of choices of things to buy, organizations to give to, and places to live. Let young people make their own decisions about how they want to use their money. If they write more checks than they have money to cover, tell them that they have to pay overdraft fees to the bank and bounced-check fees to the places that didn't get their money.

## Asset Connections

- Banking encourages responsibility (asset #30) as young people learn that they are the ones who need to monitor and maintain their accounts.
- When young people are treated as valued customers by bank and credit union personnel, they experience asset #7 (community values youth).

## Did You Know?

A survey of 428 high school seniors found that only 38 percent know that checking accounts require a minimum balance.[13]

## ATM Heaven

In the United States, there are more than 100,000 ATMs — five times more than the number of McDonald's restaurants in the entire world.[14]

## WRITE ABOUT IT

### TRACKING YOUR TRANSACTIONS

One way to keep track of your overall finances is to use a register similar to the kind used with savings and checking accounts. If you have access to a computer, you can use software such as Quicken or QuickBooks, which provide electronic versions of registers. Recording everything — income, money to save, money to give, and expenditures — in one place gives a person or a family a clear picture of how much money is really being accumulated and spent.

This worksheet shows an example of how this might work. Figure out the balance after each transaction and then think about how keeping a record like this could help you manage your financial situation.

| Date | Transaction | Deposit (+) | Withdrawal (–) | Balance |
|---|---|---|---|---|
| 3/1 | Opening deposit (money from a summer job) | $100.00 | | $100.00 |
| 3/1 | 10% saved to buy a 10-speed bike later on | | $10.00 | $90.00 |
| 3/1 | 10% saved for giving to Habitat for Humanity | | $10.00 | |
| 3/7 | Cash: To go out on Friday night | | $10.00 | |
| 3/8 | Weekly allowance | $5.00 | | |
| 3/8 | 10% of allowance saved to buy a 10-speed bike later on | | 50¢ | |
| 3/8 | 10% of allowance saved for giving to my congregation | | 50¢ | |
| 3/15 | Cash for snacks | | $2.00 | |
| 3/20 | Credit card charge to music CD purchase | | $20.00 | |
| 3/25 | Cash paid back to Mom for money I borrowed last month | | $5.00 | |
| 3/31 | Interest earned | $4.20 | | |

What's the total amount of income? What's the total amount saved? What's the total amount saved to give to charity? What's the total amount spent? When you look beyond the starting and closing balances, you get a better picture of the different ways you are using your money.

| Date | Transaction | Deposit (+) | Withdrawal (–) | Balance |
|---|---|---|---|---|
| 3/1 | Opening deposit (money from a summer job) | $100.00 | | $100.00 |
| 3/1 | 10% saved to buy a 10-speed bike later on | | $10.00 | $90.00 |
| 3/1 | 10% saved for giving to Habitat for Humanity | | $10.00 | $80.00 |
| 3/7 | Cash: To go out on Friday night | | $10.00 | $70.00 |
| 3/8 | Weekly allowance | $5.00 | | $75.00 |
| 3/8 | 10% of allowance saved to buy a 10-speed bike later on | | 50¢ | $74.50 |
| 3/8 | 10% of allowance saved for giving to my congregation | | 50¢ | $74.00 |
| 3/15 | Cash for snacks | | $2.00 | $72.00 |
| 3/20 | Credit card charge to music CD purchase | | $20.00 | $52.00 |
| 3/25 | Cash paid back to Mom for money I borrowed last month | | $5.00 | $47.00 |
| 3/31 | Interest earned | $4.20 | | $51.20 |

What's the total amount of income? $109.20. What's the total amount saved? $21.00. What's the total amount saved to give to charity? $10.50. What's the total amount spent? $27.00.

This page may be reproduced for educational, noncommercial uses only. From *An Asset Builder's Guide to Youth and Money* by Jolene L. Roehlkepartain. Copyright © 1999 by Search Institute, 700 South Third Street, Suite 210, Minneapolis, MN 55415; 800-888-7828; www.search-institute.org.

## Income

People get money in many different ways. Some earn it, others inherit it, win it, steal it, or receive it as gifts. This section helps you help young people explore where their money comes from, how much they think they need, how much they actually bring in, and how their values can influence the way they choose to generate income.

## Earning

In a capitalist economic system, in which the distribution of resources is based on buying and selling goods or services in a free market (meaning everyone has a chance to participate), most income comes from earnings — payment for labor or products.

There are two ways of thinking about how you want to earn money. The first is to figure out how much you want to have and then look for a job or career that will probably pay that much. The second approach is to think about what you like to do, what you are good at, what impact you hope to have, and then explore what kinds of jobs or careers can build on these strengths, interests, and goals. Part of the second approach includes thinking about the balance you hope to have in your life between things you do for pay and things you do for other reasons. For example, some teenagers choose not to work or to limit their hours because they believe they need to spend a lot of time on homework, in other activities, and with family and friends. Similarly, some adults pursue jobs or careers that allow them to spend time with family, volunteering, or in other ways that are important to them but don't involve pay.

Ideally, the times when people have to do work that they don't like or don't want to do are limited. Working can bring more than just a paycheck. It can enrich your life by building skills, by allowing you to interact with interesting people, by challenging you in stimulating ways, and by preparing you for future employment and a career. So before deciding to pursue a job or increase your hours, think about your life goals and how the way you earn reflects those goals.

 **Think about It**

- Are you happy with how much time you spend earning money? Why or why not?
- Are you happy with how much you earn? Why or why not?
- When you think about earning money now or in the future, do you focus more on how much you want to earn or how you want to earn it? Why is this so?
- If you could easily earn as much money as you needed and wanted, how would that change your life?
- Do you think there are enough opportunities in your community for young people to earn money?
- What other earning opportunities do you think there should be for young people?
- How can you bring together what you know, what you want to do, and who you want to be in a way that can generate income?

 **Try It**

- Bring a large jar full of pennies to your group. Explain that for about three minutes each person is going to try and get as many pennies as possible. Tell them that they can hoard, steal, negotiate, trade, or do anything else (except hurt someone) to try and have the most pennies at the end of the game. Spread the pennies out on a table or on the ground. Have the young people circle around them and start trying to get them as soon as you say go. After three minutes, have people stop and count up their pennies. Then ask questions such as these: Was there a winner in this game? How do we determine who the winner is? What things did you do to try to get pennies? What was it like having everyone working against everyone else? Did any of you work out any deals for pennies? What was that like? Was it more important to you to get a lot of pennies for yourself or to make sure that everyone had some pennies? Why is that so? What was it like to see some people having a lot of pennies and others not having very many? How did it feel to hoard and not share with others? Do you think this game is like real life in any way?

- Invite a panel of adults or older teens to speak to your group. Include at least one person who worked a lot and earned a lot of money as a teen, another who didn't work at all, and another who worked some, but not a lot. Ask them to share their experiences, answer questions from the group, and give advice to the group on how to balance working with other priorities as a teenager.

- Ask each young person to list on a piece of paper three careers he or she is interested in pursuing. For each career, ask them to research three things: the education and experience needed to get that career, the starting pay for that career, and the pay of that career after 10 years of experience. Visit a library and work with a librarian to find sources that have the answers to these questions. Encourage young people to find out accurate information about the earnings based on their gender and their ethnicity, because although many people are working to end economic inequality, in general women still earn less than men and people of color still earn less than whites in similar jobs.

## Asset Connections

- Family support (asset #1) and family boundaries (asset #11) are important in money matters, particularly earnings. Young people and their parent(s) or guardian(s) may have totally different expectations.
- Earning money can greatly impact the constructive-use-of-time assets (assets #17–20) as young people balance earning money with time spent in creative activities, cocurricular clubs or programs, youth programs, religious institutions, and time at home.

## Did You Know?

Nearly one-half (48%) of teenagers say they get money from their parents. Here's where else they say it comes from:[15]

| Occasional jobs | 43% |
| Regular allowance | 33% |
| Part-time jobs | 30% |
| Full-time jobs | 13% |

## Allowances: How Much Young People Get

Of young people who receive an allowance, 8th graders get an average of $10 a week, 10th graders average $15 a week, and 12th graders average $18 a week.[16]

**WRITE ABOUT IT**

# WHERE YOUR MONEY COMES FROM

Do you have a pretty good idea of how much money you take in over a year? Do you know where your money is coming from? If you take the time to figure it out, you may be surprised. Use this worksheet to help you think about and add up your different sources of income.

| Money Source | How Often You Receive It | Amount You Typically Receive |
|---|---|---|
| Allowance | | |
| Gifts (birthdays, holidays, etc.) | | |
| Extra jobs around where you live (washing a car, cleaning, preparing meals, watching younger family members) | | |
| Extra jobs for neighbors or friends (baby-sitting, lawn mowing, shoveling walks, pet walking or sitting, picking up mail and newspapers when neighbors are gone) | | |
| Part-time job | | |
| Things you make or services you sell to friends (making friendship bracelets, providing tutoring, making greeting cards) | | |
| Running a small business (creating Web sites, repairing bikes, gardening, selling fruits and vegetables from your garden) | | |
| Other (specify): _____ _____ _____ | | |

The next time you earn some money or receive it as a gift, set it aside for a certain amount of time (such as one week) before using it. What happens when you slow down your use of the money you receive?

This page may be reproduced for educational, noncommercial uses only. From *An Asset Builder's Guide to Youth and Money* by Jolene L. Roehlkepartain. Copyright © 1999 by Search Institute, 700 South Third Street, Suite 210, Minneapolis, MN 55415; 800-888-7828; www.search-institute.org.

## Being an Entrepreneur

Young people are finding that when they combine their skills with their passions, they can launch successful companies and make money doing what they enjoy. That's what 15-year-old Matt Boch has done. He designs personalized Web pages for clients, charging $200 to $500 a job. "Some people assume that just because you're young you don't have knowledge," he says about starting his own company, Hit Me! Web Design. "But once you earn their trust, it's easier."

The Department of Labor says that the number of 16- to 19-year-olds working in the computer and data-processing industry soared from 5,000 in 1994 to 29,000 in 1998.[17] Many young people use the Internet to market themselves around the nation and even the world.

Technology isn't the only area that's open to young entrepreneurs (people who start their own businesses). Young people are also running greeting card companies, jewelry-making companies, tutoring services, data-processing services, among others. Some young people have even taken more traditional jobs and expanded them. For example, one group of teenage girls created a child-care co-op in which they work together to provide more services and flexibility by letting clients know that at least one of the sitters is available most of the time.

For most people, being an entrepreneur is a way to use personal skills and interests to make money. What you gain isn't necessarily a sizable income (although sometimes it is). You also get important hands-on experience in working for yourself to provide services or products for others. Being an entrepreneur is a way to manage, organize, and take responsibility for something you've created or developed. It's a way to make money *and* be who you want to be and do what you want to do.

 **Think about It**

- Do you know of any teen or adult entrepreneurs? What do you think about the risks they've taken in starting their own business. Do you admire them? Why or why not?
- What skills do you think are most important in being a successful entrepreneur?
- Are there ways in which you are or have been entrepreneurial?
- If you were to start your own business, what would it be? Why?
- What scares you about being an entrepreneur? What excites you? What inspires you?

 **Try It**

- Encourage young people to take on a project that gives them a chance to act as entrepreneurs. For example, as a fund-raiser, hold an auction where young people put their time and talents to work for the highest bidder. Invite all young people in your organization to offer time or talents such as writing a story, song, or poem; baby-sitting; cooking a meal; serenading someone; building a birdhouse; giving a car an oil change; raking a lawn; running errands (for teenagers with cars); or bathing and walking a dog.
- Help young people develop entrepreneurial skills by involving them in leadership and responsibility in all areas or your organization, including planning, visioning, publicizing, recruiting, developing action plans and tasks, evaluating, leading meetings, and organizing events. Or, involve them in a specific youth-led service project or special event. A resource that gives some helpful tips on involving youth in leadership is *Youth Governance: 14 Points to Involving Young People Successfully on Boards of Directors* by Jenny Sazama (available from Youth on Board, 58 Day Street, Sommerville, MA 02144; 617-623-9900).

- Invite teen entrepreneurs or a young person from Junior Achievement to talk with your group about their experiences. Encourage your group to brainstorm a list of questions, such as, When did you get started? Why did you start? What has been difficult about being an entrepreneur? What do you enjoy most about it? What situations — positive or negative — have you experienced because of your age? If you were to start over again, what would you do differently? What advice would you give other young people who want to become entrepreneurs?

### Asset Connections

- When young people combine their interests and skills to provide an entrepreneurial service or product, they find an empowering, useful role, which asset #8 (youth as resources) is all about.
- Young people who enjoy their entrepreneurial work often feel motivated to achieve (asset #21).

### Did You Know?

You don't need to have a lot of money to start a business. Being an entrepreneur can be as simple as getting the word out about your services. Things you can do that don't cost money include dog walking, pet-sitting, lawn mowing (if you already have a mower), running errands, and baby-sitting.

### The Benefits of Extracurricular Activities

Developing the skills to be an entrepreneur is more likely to come through extracurricular activities than part-time jobs during the teenage years, say researchers Ellen Greenberger and Laurence Steinberg. These activities give young people skills in leadership and academic success while enhancing their ambition to do well in their future careers.[18]

**WRITE ABOUT IT**

# GETTING STARTED AS AN ENTREPRENEUR

It takes planning to develop a successful business. Use this form to help you think about and plan for a business you might like to create. Depending on the type of business, you'll probably have to do a little research to find the answers.

Your business name: _____
_____
_____

A one-sentence description: _____
_____
_____
_____

The product or service you will provide: _____
_____
_____
_____

Supplies you'll need: _____
_____
_____
_____

Number of hours you plan to spend on your business each week: _____
_____
_____

The amount of money you need to invest in order to start: _____
_____
_____

Names of possible clients or buyers: _____
_____
_____
_____

How big do you think the need is for the product or service you'd like to provide? What other entrepreneurs do you know who could give you some pointers on getting starting? How would your business fit in with the other activities of your life?

This page may be reproduced for educational, noncommercial uses only. From *An Asset Builder's Guide to Youth and Money* by Jolene L. Roehlkepartain. Copyright © 1999 by Search Institute, 700 South Third Street, Suite 210, Minneapolis, MN 55415; 800-888-7828; www.search-institute.org.

## Saving

There are many important reasons to save. Being able to buy something is one, but the security it provides is even more crucial. Having money in savings can help in unexpected situations such as the loss of a job, a health-care emergency, or necessary household repairs. Savings can also be used for special events such as vacations, parties or celebrations, or expensive outings. This section deals with the basics of saving, investing as a way of saving, and the connections between saving and dealing with debt.

### The Basics of Saving

Some people must just be natural savers. From the time they are very small, these people save their favorite food until the end of the meal, they save their allowance to buy something big rather than spending it right away, and they even save the toys they grow out of, knowing that someone else might want them someday. But for most people, saving is the budgetary item that is cut back on when money is tight. The average American saves only 2 to 5 percent of her or his earnings. That means of every $100 earned, only $2 to $5 is saved. Those who earn $10,000 save only $200 to $500. Financial experts say this isn't nearly enough.[19]

Saving money has benefits beyond just keeping money tucked away in case you need it. If you choose to put the money you save into some kind of account with a financial institution, you'll earn interest on it. A savings account at a bank is the most common way to do this, but other types of accounts (such as investments) can also be a means for saving.

Having money to save requires a new frame of mind for many people: to think of living *beneath* your means or, in other words, to be content with spending less than the money you bring in. Saving also requires the self-discipline to develop a plan or goal and stick with it. You'll never save money if you don't first have an attitude of saving and then have the discipline to follow through with setting aside a certain portion of your income.

Another way to think of savings is to look at the big picture of your financial goals and plans. Examining your savings along with your spending and giving can often give you a clearer idea of where you want to go. Saving will sound less overwhelming when you focus on the big picture, such as saving 10 percent, giving 10 percent, and spending 80 percent. When you keep the big picture in mind, it reminds you that most of the money is being used for spending.

### Think about It

- Who makes the decisions about savings in your family? How have these decisions affected your attitude toward saving money?
- Do you try to save some of your money? Why?
- What are your savings goals? (If you don't have any, what might some of those goals be?)
- What keeps you from achieving your saving goals?
- What one small thing can you do to challenge yourself to meet your savings goals?

### Try It

- Give every young person an envelope. Challenge them to save as much money as they can over a period of time (such as a week or month) and to keep the money in the envelope. When the time has passed, have each person figure out the totals in her or his envelope, but keep it confidential. Without talking about how much each person has, discuss questions such as these: Did it make a difference to you to have a specific place to put your savings? Did you have a goal for yourself? Did you achieve that goal? Were you surprised by how much you saved?

Why or why not? What will you do with the money you saved?

■ Visit a local bank or credit union and ask an employee to explain what's required for opening a savings account. (Many banks offer savings accounts for young people that don't have a minimum deposit.) Brainstorm a list of questions before the visit and encourage everyone to ask these questions and others that come to mind during the visit.

■ Ask young people to share some of their saving techniques with each other. Encourage them to talk about the method, not the amount saved. For example, some people save any money that they find, including pennies. Others spend only dollar bills and save all their change in a jar or box. Some save money they're given as gifts and spend it once they reach a certain amount. If young people don't have many suggestions, have a group brainstorm to help them think creatively.

## Asset Connections

■ Saving is about having asset #40 (positive view of personal future). When young people save, they are thinking about the future and planning ways to make it how they want it to be.

■ Saving entails taking responsibility (asset #30). Young people cannot save unless they have the discipline to set money aside, even when they don't want to.

■ According to Search Institute research, the more assets young people have, the more likely they are to say they save money for something special rather than spending it all right away.

## Did You Know?

Most young people believe that a bank savings account is the safest place for their money. Eighty-six percent of young people choose a bank savings account over stocks, corporate bonds, and locking the money in a closet at home. On the other hand, few young people could identify which would most likely have the highest growth over the next 18 years. In choosing between savings accounts, checking accounts, U.S. government savings bonds, and stocks, only 15 percent correctly identified stocks as the answer.[20]

## To Start Saving: Start Small

If you've never saved before, you might want to ease into it. "Put one percent of [your income] in a savings account this month," says Nancy Dunnan, author of *How to Invest $50 to $5000*. "Then increase that percentage by one percent each month for up to a year."[21] If a monthly increase seems too difficult, try a quarterly increase, a semiannual increase, or an annual increase.

## WRITE ABOUT IT

# YOUR SAVINGS GOAL

Saving money takes time, but more important, it takes planning. Think about how much money you'd like to save, either to buy something (a new jacket, for example) or have the security of money in the bank. Write the total amount you'd like to save next to the dollar sign across from the 100% mark on the savings scale below. Then figure out the other percentage amounts and write in those dollar goals. After you finish, think about a reward for each savings achievement. Make sure the rewards do not involve spending money. See the "Other Ideas for Rewards" list to get you thinking. Then start saving. Chart your progress by coloring the goals you reach, one by one. And see what happens.

**Success!**

- 100%  $ _____ Reward:
- 75%   $ _____ Reward:
- 50%   $ _____ Reward:
- 30%   $ _____ Reward:
- 15%   $ _____ Reward:
- 5%    $ _____ Reward:
- 0%    $    0

**Example**

- 100%  $ 50.00  Reward: Buy that jacket you've been saving for.
- 75%   $ 37.50  Reward: Set aside a block of time one day to do only the favorite things you want to do.
- 50%   $ 25.00  Reward: Fly a kite in a park with one of your friends.
- 30%   $ 15.00  Reward: Talk on the phone with your best friend for two straight hours one weekend.
- 15%   $ 7.50   Reward: Spend a weekend afternoon reading your favorite book.
- 5%    $ 2.50   Reward: Go biking on your favorite bike trail.
- 0%    $    0

### OTHER IDEAS FOR REWARDS

- Bake yourself something good to eat.
- Go for a walk in a park (or on your favorite hiking trail).
- Invite a friend to sleep over (after you get permission from your parent[s] or guardian[s]).
- Ask your parent(s) or guardian(s) to extend your curfew by one hour on one weekend.
- Check out a music CD from your local library. What motivates you to save? What could entice you to stretch your savings rate from where it is now?

---

This page may be reproduced for educational, noncommercial uses only. From *An Asset Builder's Guide to Youth and Money* by Jolene L. Roehlkepartain. Copyright © 1999 by Search Institute, 700 South Third Street, Suite 210, Minneapolis, MN 55415; 800-888-7828; www.search-institute.org.

## Part 2: Core Money Management Issues

### Investing

In financial terms, investing means using your money to support an enterprise (such as a new business) with the hope that you will get even more money in return when the enterprise generates a profit. Some people think of investments as a source of income. But they are really more of a way of saving. That's because investments generally earn money in the long run, but there can be many ups and downs in between. To get the most out of investing, you need to think of it as setting the money aside and leaving it there for a long time (at least 5 years).

There are many ways to invest—through a person who specializes in managing investments (a broker), over the Internet, or through an investment company. Although you don't need to know all the details, it's important to do enough research to know the basics of how investments work and what kinds of companies you might want to invest in. Some people choose companies or funds that they think will make a lot of money. Other investors choose those that have practices and policies that are consistent with their values (such as not manufacturing or selling tobacco products); these are generally referred to as "social-investment funds."

In addition to knowing the basics of investing and the kinds of investments you're interested in, it's also important to know how much money you are willing to lose. Investments don't guarantee a profit, and there are people who have lost money on them because the enterprise was not successful. So it's not a good idea to put all of your money in one or two companies or funds. On the other hand, many financial planners say that it's virtually impossible for people to achieve their financial goals without investing at least some of their money. This is largely because people are living longer, inflation is higher (meaning prices are higher), company retirement plans pay less than they did in decades past, and many people want to retire early.[22]

### Think about It

- Do you know anyone who invests money for the long term? Who? How have they made their decisions to invest?
- Do investments seem like a good way for you to save money for the future? Why or why not?
- At what age do you think you should start investing?
- What kinds of companies would you like to invest in? Why?

### Try It

- Help young people learn the language of investing. Start by taking the What's What of Investment Terms quiz on page 37. Most likely, few young people will be familiar with these terms. Take time to talk about and become familiar with them.
- Have each young person choose one mutual fund and one individual stock from the New York Stock Exchange to follow over a period of time on a daily or weekly basis. (Ideally, it would be best to do this on a weekly basis over a two- to three-month period to teach young people the concept of long-term investing and not to panic when the fund or stock suffers a large loss one day and then recovers later.) Have young people invest an imaginary $100 and keep track of the closing price of the fund or stock for each period. Have them regularly check the worth of each fund and stock and see who has the largest gain and the largest loss by the end of your designated period.
- If there's an investment club in your community, invite a representative to talk about what they do and who participates. As a group, brainstorm questions for your young people to ask the person. Include questions about her or his positive and negative investing experiences.
- Financial experts say that there are basically two types of investments: stocks (which also includes

mutual funds) and interest-earning investments.[23] Have young people work (either individually or in pairs) to find out about a specific investment within one of these two categories.

- Divide your group into two teams. Ask one team to research the concept of automatic investing and the other to research dollar-cost averaging. These are two key elements of investing. After they have gathered the information, ask for representatives from each team to report what they found out.

- Help young people gather information on regular mutual funds and social-investment funds. Three general mutual funds that allow for small initial investments include Twentieth Century Investors (800-345-2021), the Janus Fund (800-525-3713), and United Services (800-873-8637).[24] Some social-investment funds include Working Assets (800-533-3863), Calvert (800-368-2745), and Pax World (800-767-1729).[25] There are also Internet resources with information on funds. Encourage young people to compare the types of companies that each fund invests in. After they have gathered the information, discuss the differences they found between general mutual funds and social investment funds.

## Asset Connections

- Investing requires having a positive view of one's personal future (asset #40).

- People who purchase social investments (mutual funds that invest in companies that promote human rights, animal rights, equality, health, environmental protection, and other concerns) are acting on the positive-value assets of equality and social justice (asset #27) and integrity (asset #28: acting on convictions).

## Did You Know?

If you set aside $100 today, after three decades you'd have $100 if you kept the money in a drawer, you'd have an estimated $712 if you kept it in a savings account, and you'd have $1,871 if you invested it in the stock market.[26]

## Handling the Downside of Investments

"A decline in stocks is not a surprising event, it's a recurrent event — as normal as frigid air in Minnesota," says Peter Lynch, former fund manager of Fidelity Magellan, who is seen as the leading successful expert on investments. "You put on your parka, throw salt on the walk, and remind yourself that by summertime, it will be warm outside. A successful investor has the same relationship with a drop in the market as a Minnesotan has with freezing weather. You know it's coming and you're ready to ride it out."[27]

Part 2: Core Money Management Issues

## WRITE ABOUT IT

### RIDING THE UPS AND DOWNS OF INVESTMENTS

Investments should be viewed as a long-term commitment because there can be a lot of fluctuation in their value; most, however, increase over time. The good news when prices go down is that if you want to invest more, you can get more shares for your money. Use this worksheet to get an idea of how long it might take to see a payoff on an investment.

| Date | Amount Invested | Price per Share | Number of Shares Purchased (divide the amount invested by the price per share) | Total Shares Owned (add the number of shares purchased to the total shares owned from the previous transaction) | Net Worth of Stock (multiply the price per share by the total number of shares owned) |
|---|---|---|---|---|---|
| 5-1-99 | $0 | $14.70 | 0 | 0 | 0 |
| 5-15-99 | $100 | $14.75 | 6.779661 | 6.779661 | $100.00 |
| 6-15-99 | $100 | $14.00 | 7.1428571 | 13.922518 | $194.92 |
| 7-15-99 | $100 | $13.75 | | | |
| 8-15-99 | $100 | $14.25 | | | |
| 9-15-99 | $100 | $14.75 | | | |
| 10-15-99 | $100 | $15.00 | | | |
| 11-15-99 | $100 | $15.10 | | | |
| 12-15-99 | $100 | $15.30 | | | |
| 1-15-00 | $100 | $15.60 | | | |

It wasn't until the August 15, 1999, investment was made that you actually began to earn money, which is why some people have a hard time psychologically with investing in stocks and bonds. They focus on the fact that they lost money with the June 15 and the July 15 deposits. Yet, look at your earnings by January 15. You had a 6 percent return on your investment, which is two to three percentage points higher than if you had saved the money in a savings account at a bank. However, this still is too early to decide whether this was a good investment or not.

Say you decided not to invest any more money and the number of your total shares froze at 61.2227838. Imagine that the stock market took a hit on July 15, 2000, and the price per share dropped to $12.00. How much would your total investment be worth? How much would you have lost? Say you didn't panic and sell when the stock market dropped but decided to ride out the fall. If one year later, on July 15, 2001, the stock market boomed and the price per share rose to $21.75, how much would the net worth of your shares be? How much would you have earned overall?

| Date | Amount Invested | Price per Share | Number of Shares Purchased | Total Shares Owned | Net Worth of Stock |
|---|---|---|---|---|---|
| 5-1-99 | $0 | $14.70 | 0 | 0 | 0 |
| 5-15-99 | $100 | $14.75 | 6.779661 | 6.779661 | $100.00 |
| 6-15-99 | $100 | $14.00 | 7.1428571 | 13.922518 | $194.92 |
| 7-15-99 | $100 | $13.75 | 7.2727273 | 21.195245 | $291.43 |
| 8-15-99 | $100 | $14.25 | 7.0175439 | 28.212789 | $402.03 |
| 9-15-99 | $100 | $14.75 | 6.779661 | 34.99245 | $516.14 |
| 10-15-99 | $100 | $15.00 | 6.6666667 | 41.659117 | $624.89 |
| 11-15-99 | $100 | $15.10 | 6.6225166 | 48.281634 | $729.05 |
| 12-15-99 | $100 | $15.30 | 6.5359477 | 54.817582 | $838.71 |
| 1-15-00 | $100 | $15.60 | 6.4102564 | 61.2227838 | $955.15 |

On July 15, 2000, your investment would be worth $734.67. Your loss would be $900 (which is the total amount you've invested through those monthly deposits) minus $734.67, which would give you a loss of $165.33.

On July 15, 2001, the investment would be worth $1,331.60. Your net gain (from your initial $900 investment) would be $431.60, which is equal to almost half of your initial investment. Your investment did very well.

This page may be reproduced for educational, noncommercial uses only. From *An Asset Builder's Guide to Youth and Money* by Jolene L. Roehlkepartain. Copyright © 1999 by Search Institute, 700 South Third Street, Suite 210, Minneapolis, MN 55415; 800-888-7828; www.search-institute.org.

# WRITE ABOUT IT

## THE WHAT'S WHAT OF INVESTMENT TERMS

Match each investment term and concept on the left with its definition on the right.

**1. New York Stock Exchange** _____ **A.** The price of a single stock or mutual fund share.

**2. Certificates of deposit** _____ **B.** A person who buys stocks, bonds, or mutual funds.

**3. Automatic investing** _____ **C.** The price of the investment at the end of the trading day.

**4. Fund** _____ **D.** An investment that buys you a portion, or share, of a specific company or corporation.

**5. Share** _____ **E.** Where stocks of most major U.S. companies are traded (also known as "Wall Street").

**6. Bond** _____ **F.** The current financial worth of your total shares of an investment.

**7. Dollar-cost averaging** _____ **G.** A mixture of investments that represent a number of different companies or types of businesses.

**8. Closing price** _____ **H.** Investing money on a regular basis (such as monthly or quarterly) through an automatic transfer from another type of account.

**9. Stock** _____ **I.** A loan you make to a bank for a specific amount of time (such as 2, 5, or 10 years). The bank invests the money and agrees to pay back the loan plus a predetermined amount of interest at the end of the time.

**10. Investor** _____ **J.** Another name for a mutual fund.

**11. Net worth of a stock** _____ **K.** One part of an investment, into which a stock or mutual fund is divided equally.

**12. Social-investment funds** _____ **L.** The average cost per share, figured annually on an investment that has been purchased on a regular basis (such as monthly or quarterly).

**13. Mutual Fund** _____ **M.** A certificate showing that you have loaned, with interest, a specific amount of money to a corporation or government security.

**14. Price per share** _____ **N.** Mutual funds that do not invest in companies that manufacture or sell certain types of products (such as weapons or tobacco) or engage in certain practices (such as animal testing or violating human rights).

ANSWERS: 1. E; 2. I; 3. H; 4. J; 5. K; 6. M; 7. L; 8. C; 9. D; 10. B; 11. F; 12. N; 13. G; 14. A.

This page may be reproduced for educational, noncommercial uses only. From *An Asset Builder's Guide to Youth and Money* by Jolene L. Roehlkepartain. Copyright © 1999 by Search Institute, 700 South Third Street, Suite 210, Minneapolis, MN 55415; 800-888-7828; www.search-institute.org.

# Giving

Nurturing a commitment to supporting people and causes through financial giving sets young people on a life course toward being generous, thoughtful, responsible members of society. Teaching them how to make decisions about how much to give and to whom can help them make a difference in ways that are important to them. This section focuses on introducing the topic to young people, charitable giving, giving to religious organizations, giving gifts, using fund-raisers to gather more money to give than an individual could on her or his own, and grant making.

## Introducing Giving

Giving and serving are concepts that are often linked and addressed together because both are usually motivated by a desire to help others (asset #26) and to make a positive difference in the world.

However, while much is understood about young people's commitment to service and the types of programs that work best to engage them, little is known about why and how young people give money away. Even less is known about how to nurture these habits. What is known is that people who get involved in serving and volunteerism early in life are more likely to continue those practices later on.[28] It's likely that the same is true of giving.

Some people are not comfortable asking others to give money. But once people see the power their money can have, they are often convinced of the importance of giving. Even just 1 percent of your weekly income can make a difference because when many people give small amounts they add up and people and organizations benefit. Even a few nickels and dimes matter to the organization that receives them. "Sometimes we get [from young people] contributions of quarters taped to a piece of paper," says Jon Hockman, director of special events at the Children's Defense Fund in Washington, D.C. He says when he receives those donations it is clear that young people really want to give.[29]

Ideally, giving becomes not a one-time event but something that people do on a consistent basis. For some, giving money during holidays each year is how they start. For others, giving monthly or weekly is a way they can get into the habit. What's important is to figure out what works best for you and to start doing it. Don't ever feel embarrassed by how much or how little you have to give.

### Think about It

- Do your parent(s) or guardian(s) give money to organizations or causes they care about? How about your grandparents? Other family members? Does your family have norms or expectations about giving money?
- How have your family's beliefs affected your beliefs about giving money?
- What has been your personal history of giving money? How has that experience shaped your current giving habits?
- Do you think everyone should give some money away? If so, what are the minimum standards for giving, such as what age to start, the least amount a person should give, and want level of income a person should have in order to give?
- What keeps you from giving — or giving more than you already do?

### Try It

- Play the game of Monopoly with a twist. The goal is for each player is to own only one set of property, have $2,000 in the bank, and give away as much as possible to other players who are having a hard time reaching that goal. (If you have a large group, set up a number of these games with about four to six players in each.) Afterward, ask questions such as these: How does playing the game feel different than if you've played it to own as much as you can and have as much money as you can at the expense of the other players? Which version of the game do you like better? Why? If this new version were sold in this country, would it be popular? Why or why not?

- Read this true story to your group: "When Eleanor Boyer won $8.5 million in the state lottery, she essentially gave away the entire amount she won. Half went to her congregation and the other half went to charities. 'I have everything I need,' 73-year-old Boyer says. Despite the winnings, she still drives the same 1969 Chevy Malibu with a peeling vinyl roof. 'Why let the money sit in the bank till I die?'"[30] Then discuss the story. Ask questions such as these: What do you think about this woman giving away everything she won? What do you think about the way she got the money? Why do you think she gave it all away and didn't buy herself a new car or some other things that she probably wanted? Why do you think she bought a lottery ticket if she didn't want the money? If you received $8.5 million, would you give away some or all of it? Why?

- Have young people research the giving habits of their heroes. For example, magazine articles and books often mention how celebrities such as basketball player Shaquille O'Neal, country singer LeAnn Rimes, baseball player Mark McGwire, and pop singer Whitney Houston donate their time and money. A librarian also can give assistance in helping young people identify resources that will help them find this information.

## Asset Connections

- Giving money to support school functions can be a way to bond to your school (asset #24). It also is a way to bond to a youth organization, a community, an organization you believe in, or a congregation.
- Giving can build asset #27 (equality and social justice), especially when young people choose to give money to charities that work to reduce hunger and poverty or promote human rights. Giving also can build cultural competence (asset #34) if young people give to groups that promote tolerance, equality, understanding, and cooperation among different cultural, racial, and ethnic groups.

## Did You Know?

About half of all financial giving occurs during the months of November and December, when people think about giving for the winter holidays and making last-minute charitable tax deductions.[31]

## Big Givers?

People generally give more as they get older according to one study. The percentages of people within different age-groups who give money to charity during the winter holidays are as follows:

| | |
|---|---|
| 18- to 34-year-olds | 61% |
| 35- to 54-year-olds | 76% |
| 55-year-olds and older | 79%[32] |

## Part 2: Core Money Management Issues

### WRITE ABOUT IT
### MAKING A DIFFERENCE THROUGH GIVING

Multibillionaire businessman Ted Turner gave $1 billion to the United Nations. Hearing stories like that can make giving away a few dollars seem pointless or at least insignificant. But people have different needs, different means, and different priorities. How much you give is not as important as *whether* you give.

To get you thinking about the ways you have given and new ways you'd like to try, look at this list of ways to serve others with your money. Circle those you have done in the past. Place a star next to the thing you'd like to do next.

- Help with a fund-raiser.

- Buy a card, flower, or some other token of encouragement to give to someone who is having a hard time.

- Give money to someone without expecting the person to pay you back.

- Give money to a charity.

- Give money to a congregation.

- Give money to a good cause.

- Buy an item that others sell to raise money.

- Save a certain percentage of your money during the year to donate to a worthy cause at the end of the year.

- Pitch in money to buy a group present for someone.

- Donate money to a cause *before* anyone asks you to.

- Take someone out and treat that person to an ice cream cone, coffee, or soda — just for fun.

- Buy an item that is produced in an ecologically or socially beneficial way.

- Donate money to someone else doing a fund-raiser.

- Take time off from working (such as baby-sitting or another part-time job) to volunteer your time to help someone.

- Shop at businesses that support economically depressed neighborhoods or communities.

- Give money anonymously.

- Shop at a nonprofit store that benefits people with disabilities or helps people become economically self-sufficient.

If you like to focus on quantity, think about the total number of experiences you can create for yourself to give money away, instead of thinking about the amount that you give each time. For example, some people prefer donating money to five different organizations (even though they may give only $2 to each organization) instead of choosing just one.

## Charitable Giving

There are many different types of giving. Charitable giving means supporting organizations, causes, or people who rely on donated funds. Issues that can be addressed through charitable giving can include hunger, homelessness, animal rights, the arts, education, the environment, health and human services, international affairs, recreation, and youth development. In fact, if you're willing to do a little research, you can probably find at least one charitable organization to contribute to that ties into your interests, concerns, and values.

Charitable giving by individuals accounts for a lot of the good things that happen in our society, including programs and services that otherwise might not be available. So when you contribute to charitable organizations, you're showing what's important to you. You're taking a stand by using your money in ways that support your long-term goals, interests, and concerns. Giving money to charity can help you develop habits of generosity that will accompany you throughout your life. And these lifelong habits can give you a great sense of personal satisfaction and power to make a difference.

### Think about It

- Have you ever given money to a charitable organization? If not, why not? If you have made such contributions, what motivated you? How did you feel afterward?
- Are there things that make it difficult to give to charity? What are they?
- If you had $1,000 to give away, who or what would you give it to and why?
- How have you seen adults model giving money to charity? What have you learned?
- Are you more likely to give in times of crisis (such as during wars, floods, or natural disasters) or to meet ongoing needs (such as for food or affordable housing)? Why?

### Try It

- Request a free copy of the current *Wise Giving Guide* from the National Charities Information Bureau (NCIB). (Or as a group, have each young person request her or his own copy.) You can make the request through the NCIB's Web page (http://www.give.org) or by mail (National Charities Information Bureau, Department 9702, 19 Union Square West, New York, NY 10003). Once you receive the guide, have young people choose four organizations from the list that they might be interested in supporting financially. Have each person explain to the others her or his choices. As a group, talk about the value of researching organizations before making any contributions, since the NCIB says that each year $1 billion that people give goes directly to scam organizations.[33] The *Wise Giving Guide* helps young people spot fraudulent charities.
- Challenge young people to give money in the next month (even if it's a very small amount) to one charitable organization they have never supported before. After the month has passed, ask young people to report whether or not they gave, how they felt about it, and how they chose where to give.

### Asset Connections

- Young people who donate money to charities that work to reduce hunger and poverty are promoting asset #27 (equality and social justice).
- Young people can feel a sense of purpose (asset #39) when they contribute money to charities that do work that is consistent with their values and priorities.

## Part 2: Core Money Management Issues

### ? Did You Know?

The majority of 3,500 young people who submitted essays to a newspaper on what they'd do with $1 million said they would give some money to charity to help those less fortunate than themselves.[34]

### $ What Teenagers Give

In a national survey of giving and volunteering habits, two out of five 12- to 17-year-olds said they give money to charitable organizations. The average contribution reported by teenagers in general (which includes young people who don't do service) is $34 a year. Teenagers who also volunteer give even more—an average of $82 a year.[35]

## WRITE ABOUT IT

# GIVING MONEY TO CHARITY

If you were to give money to charity, what kind of organizations would you choose? Rank the nine types of organizations listed below in order of your priority or interest, giving a "1" to the type of organization you're most likely to give to and a "9" to the organization you're least likely to give to.

_____ Citizen lobbies, such as Common Cause or Public Citizen

_____ Political parties or political organizations

_____ Minority group organizations, such as the NAACP

_____ Organizations concerned with population problems

_____ International relief organizations, such as UNICEF

_____ Organizations concerned with environmental problems

_____ Community charities, such as the United Way

_____ Charities to help fight diseases (cancer, heart disease)

_____ A congregation or religious organizations

In a survey of 15,876 young people, respondents ranked these organizations in reverse order with citizen lobbies receiving a "9" and congregations and religious organizations receiving a "1." Here are the percentages of young people who have given money to each of these types of organizations: citizen lobbies, 0.8%; political parties or political organizations, 1.2%; minority group organizations, 1.3%; organizations concerned with population problems, 1.9%; international relief organizations, 4.4%; organizations concerned with environmental problems, 5.5%; community charities, 6.1%; charities to help fight diseases, 10.7%; a congregation or religious organizations, 25.8%.[36]

If you're intentional about giving (and don't just give to whatever comes your way), you'll have more impact on the things you really care about. What can you do to become more intentional about giving so that it's meaningful to you?

This page may be reproduced for educational, noncommercial uses only. From *An Asset Builder's Guide to Youth and Money* by Jolene L. Roehlkepartain. Copyright © 1999 by Search Institute, 700 South Third Street, Suite 210, Minneapolis, MN 55415; 800-888-7828; www.search-institute.org.

## Giving to Religious Organizations

Young people give money to religious organizations (such as churches, mosques, synagogues, and temples) more often than any other type of organization or cause.[37] Giving money to religious organizations is unique for a number of reasons. For one thing, people tend to give to religious organizations on a regular basis versus a one-time or occasional donation to a charitable organization. In addition, there is an expectation in most religions that followers, believers, members — whatever participants are called — will help support the ongoing function of the organization, in addition to supporting charitable work done by the organization.

Many faith traditions have sacred writings that point to the importance of giving. This, combined with organizations' needs for budgeting and planning, leads many religious organizations to have formal systems for encouraging giving such as passing a collection plate, *tzedakah,* tithing, and *zakat,* as well as pledge drives and payment plans.

Giving money to religious organizations can provide a sense of belonging and investment in a community of people supporting one another and doing good work in the community. Some religious organizations emphasize peace and justice and raise funds to advocate for equality and tolerance. Others work hard to help those with inadequate food, housing, and opportunities. Part of choosing whether or not to support a religious organization is understanding the role of that organization in your own life and in your community.

### Think about It

- Is it important to give money to a religious organization or congregation that you are involved with? Why?
- Do you think most young people give to a congregation? Why or why not?
- Should young people be encouraged to give to congregations they are involved with? Why or why not? Should they be *expected* to give? Why or why not?
- What is your own experience of giving money to a congregation or religious organization?
- If you belong to a congregation, what do the sacred writings of your faith tradition say about giving?

### Try It

- Invite leaders from various faith traditions in your community (such as Jewish, Muslim, Christian, or Hindu) to share with young people how they handle giving. (Different faith traditions have different systems, experiences, and expectations.)
- Create an anonymous survey of your group to find out about young people's experience in giving money to religious organizations. Ask simple questions for easy tabulating. Post and discuss the results. Questions to consider asking: Have you ever given to a religious organization or congregation? If so, at what age did you first start giving? Do your parent(s) or guardian(s) give money to a religious organization or congregation? Do you have friends who give money to a religious organization or congregation?
- If you work with youth in a religious organization, invite people who are involved in giving (such as those from a finance, fund-raising, or stewardship committee) to talk about how the giving process works. Ask questions such as these: How much does the congregation depend on members' giving money? How do you keep track of giving? What happens when actual giving is different from the projected giving? How often do you ask members to reevaluate their giving? What types of giving campaigns work the best?

### Asset Connections

- Young people who give money to religious organizations they are involved with are being responsible (asset #30) and contributing (asset #8: youth as resources) members of the organization.

- Young people who give money to congregations they are involved with build asset #15 (positive peer influence) for other youth and children.

### ? Did You Know?

Young people who attend a religious service regularly are more apt to give money than young people who rarely attend. Fifty-seven percent of young people who attend religious services every week or nearly every week give money compared to only 31 percent of young people who attend only a few times a year.[38]

### ✳ Another Resource

If you work with young people in a congregation (or know of a congregation that would like to explore the issue of young people and giving), see *Kids Have a Lot to Give: How Congregations Can Nurture Habits of Giving and Serving for the Common Good* by Eugene C. Roehlkepartain (Minneapolis: Search Institute, 1999).

## WRITE ABOUT IT
# MAKING AN ONGOING FINANCIAL COMMITMENT

Congregations and other religious organizations rely on regular financial contributions from individuals. Some people give quarterly, others monthly, bimonthly, or weekly. Making a commitment to give money on a regular basis helps the congregation know what to expect and helps you remember when to give.

First, think about whether or not you would like to give money to a congregation, and, if you would like to, how much you would like to give over a one-year period. Then use this worksheet to figure out how much you need to give on a regular basis to meet that goal.

Name of congregation or religious organization I typically attend: _____

How often I attend: _____

The amount of money (or a percentage of my income) that I would like to give in one year: $ _____

**How often I would like to give money to this organization**    **How much I have to give each time**

❏ Quarterly (4 times per year)    _____

❏ Monthly (12 times per year)    _____

❏ Twice a month (24 times per year)    _____

❏ Weekly    _____

❏ Other (specify): _____
_____
_____
_____

Giving on a regular basis won't become a habit right away if it's something you've never done before. Sometimes you'll remember. Sometimes you won't. What can you do to help yourself get into the habit so that you'll remember more often than not?

## Giving Gifts

Gift giving is an important part of American culture. We give gifts during the holidays, at birthdays, anniversaries, to celebrate achievements, to cheer people up, and sometimes just because we feel like it.

Some people love to buy gifts, and others find it a burden. Some don't worry about how much they spend, and others fret about how much is too much and how much is not enough. One difficulty about gift giving is sorting out the motivations. Sometimes people feel obligated to give gifts because they've been invited to a party, or they've been given gifts in the past and feel they need to return the favor. Others do it because they think it will make people like them. Being clear about why you want to give someone a gift can help you make good decisions about how much to spend and what to give.

At its best, gift giving is done because the giver wants to show the receiver love, friendship, appreciation, sympathy, or kindness. "One of our more endearing human traits is our need to express our love and affections through gift giving," says David Elkind, professor of child study at Tufts University. At its worst, gift giving becomes a contest, manipulation, or burden. Young people especially may have unclear boundaries about what's appropriate in terms of gifts: "teenagers, because of their strong desire to be liked, often go overboard when they buy gifts for their friends. Some, in an effort to show the depths of their feelings, overdo the expense," says Elkind.[39]

Gift giving is one way that people show they care for one another. Knowing why you want to give, how much you have to spend, and what the receiver likes and would appreciate can help you make wise choices that will be valued by you and the person you give to.

### Think about It

- How important is it to you to buy gifts for other people? Why?
- How satisfied are you with the amount of money you spend on gifts for other people?
- Do you enjoy buying gifts for other people? Why or why not?
- Whom are you good at buying gifts for? Who is hard to buy gifts for?
- Have you ever received a gift that made you uncomfortable due to the amount of money that the person spent? What did you do?
- Do you ever give yourself gifts?
- Are there ways you can give gifts without spending money?

### Try It

- Invite a person who runs a retail store in your community to talk to the group about how much gift giving affects the store's annual sales. Before the person arrives, have the group brainstorm a list of questions, for example: What would happen to your business if everyone stopped giving gifts? Of all the holidays, which generates the most gift-giving sales? The least? Why? What do you know about the shoppers who buy gifts in your store? (For example, men and women and people of different ages often have different buying habits when it comes to gift giving.)
- At holiday times, have young people teach each other skills and crafts and encourage them to sometimes make gifts for family and friends instead of buying them. Or invite someone to teach an interesting craft that your young people would enjoy learning.
- As a group, discuss personal gift-giving habits. Ask questions such as these: Do you buy gifts for holidays? For how many people? Where does the money

come from? Do you ever buy birthday presents? Whom do you buy gifts for? Why? At what other times do you give gifts? How important is it for you to be able to buy gifts for other people? Do you like receiving gifts? Is our culture too much into gift giving? Why or why not?

### Asset Connections

- Giving gifts is one way to act on the positive value asset of caring (#26).
- Gift giving can build interpersonal competence (asset #33), which includes empathy, sensitivity, and friendship skills.

### Did You Know?

Gift giving is big business. According to the U.S. Census Bureau, there are 34,400 stores that *specialize* in selling gifts.[40]

### What Teens Spend for Gifts

Among teenagers who celebrate Christmas, girls spend an average of $197 on gifts and boys spend an average of $165.[41]

## WRITE ABOUT IT

### BETTER GIFT GIVING

Gifts can have power in relationships because they symbolize how we feel about a person, and they can give strong messages depending upon the choice of the gift. Some make people laugh. Others leave an impression because they mean a lot to the receiver.

Becoming a thoughtful gift giver means paying attention to the receiver's personality and what he or she likes. Choose one person you give gifts to at least once a year (such as a family member or friend) and write the name of that person here:_____. On the gift tags below, answer the questions about the person. These answers might give you some good ideas on what to give as a gift.

**Interests**

**Hobbies**

**Favorite causes or issues**

**Favorite store**

**Collections**

**Other ideas**

How do you feel about the amount of money you currently spend on gifts and the types of gifts you give? What small change would make gift giving more enjoyable for you?

---

This page may be reproduced for educational, noncommercial uses only. From *An Asset Builder's Guide to Youth and Money* by Jolene L. Roehlkepartain. Copyright © 1999 by Search Institute, 700 South Third Street, Suite 210, Minneapolis, MN 55415; 800-888-7828; www.search-institute.org.

## Fund-Raising

Fund-raising is one way that schools, organizations, congregations, and communities raise money to do their programming. Fund-raisers can be highly effective for generating a lot of money in a short amount of time. Many people enjoy donating money, time, or resources because it's a way of showing support for the individuals or organization involved.

But fund-raising can be more than just a way of supporting programs. It can also be a means for raising money to give away, or to use to support special projects that make a difference for others. For example, a congregational youth program could hold a special fund-raiser to support their efforts to rehabilitate homes in the community. If each young person involved contributed some money, they probably wouldn't have enough to complete an entire house. But if they held an event such as a car wash and asked for donations from people who came, they could raise a lot of money in just one afternoon.

Some people get excited about fund-raisers because they like figuring out how to persuade others to give, and they feel the money raised opens up new opportunities. Others feel overwhelmed because they don't like asking for money, or they feel that there are already too many youth fund-raisers within a school, organization, or community. Still others feel pressured to do fund-raisers that they don't enjoy or don't have the skills for. But no matter how you feel about fund-raisers, if you work with young people you may have to be involved in one at some point, because many organizations and schools are dependent upon them. Without fund-raisers, a team may not have uniforms or a club may not be able to take its annual camping and service trip.

The most successful fund-raisers are ones that young people enjoy doing and to which the target audience enjoys contributing. Sometimes that means a fund-raiser needs a creative twist to breathe life into it (such as a special concert where the musicians donate their time), or needs to occur at a time of year when competition with other fund-raisers is lower. "Fund raising is a big task," says Margaret Hinchey, author of *Fund-Raisers That Work*. "But remember, part of FUNd raising is FUN!"[42]

### Think about It

- What is the most creative or interesting fund-raiser you've heard of?
- What is the most boring fund-raiser you've heard of?
- What do you do fund-raisers for (or have done fund-raisers for in the past)?
- Do you enjoy doing fund-raisers? Why or why not?
- Do you think schools, organizations, and clubs should require young people to participate in fund-raisers? Why or why not?
- Do you think fund-raisers are a good way to raise money for a charitable cause, organization, or group?

### Try It

- In coming up with ideas for fund-raisers, it's often easy to think about the obvious such as car washes and bake sales. If your group is tired of doing the same old things, have a group brainstorm with only one rule: the ideas have to be things you've never done before. On paper from a flip chart, create three columns: sales, services, and special events. Write ideas under each of these categories, such as sales (homemade bread, box sale for when young people go off to college and have a hard time finding packing boxes, T-shirt sales), services (baby-sitting, painting, dog bathing), and special events (Halloween haunted house, craft fair, roller-skate-a-thon). Afterward, talk about the ideas as well as things you've done in the past and decide whether or not you want to try something new.
- Discuss ways to make a fund-raiser memorable — and newsworthy. For example, the YMCA of Seattle

created a pile of coins that caught the attention not only of those in the community but also *The Guinness Book of World Records*. The YMCA ended up collecting 1,000,298 pennies, nickels, dimes, and quarters that totaled $126,463.61.[43] Even if you don't want to set your sights on breaking a world record, you can create a fund-raiser that gets people talking and, more important, giving.

- As a group, talk about people's individual talents and interests and the expectations regarding fund-raisers. For example, some young people feel uncomfortable trying to sell things to other people. Others enjoy it. Talk about the different roles that are needed and how each person can contribute in a way that's fun for her or him. Give young people the opportunity to practice financial skills when doing a group fund-raiser. For example, planning, budgeting, setting goals, and tracking income and expenses are all essential parts of fund-raisers.

## Asset Connections

- Fund-raisers can be designed to nurture asset #3 (other adult relationships) and asset #15 (positive peer influence) by encouraging adults and youth to work in pairs or small teams.
- Building a caring neighborhood (asset #4) can be a benefit of fund-raisers that engage young people in talking with their neighbors about what they are raising money for and why. Neighbors can also be recruited to help out. If your fund-raiser involves young people interacting with people they don't know, ensure asset #10 (safety) by always having young people work in teams.

## Did You Know?

For reasons of safety, the National Parent Teacher Association (PTA) wants to ban door-to-door fund-raising sales done by young people. For groups that do choose to go door to door, the National Center for Missing and Exploited Children recommends these safety precautions:

- Don't go alone. Always bring a buddy.
- Have an adult leader nearby, at least within line-of-sight range.
- Sell only in your own community, preferably to neighbors you know by sight.[44]

## Keys to Successful Fund-Raising

Margaret Hinchey, author of *Fund Raisers That Work*, suggests these key ingredients for successful fund-raisers:

1. Empower young people. A successful fund-raiser is a youth fund-raiser, not a youth leader's fund-raiser.
2. Prepare, prepare, prepare. Get the materials and facilities you need.
3. Enlist help. Make sure you have enough people to carry out the fund-raiser.
4. Have adequate adult supervision.[45]

**WRITE ABOUT IT**

## FUND-RAISER PRESELECTION EVALUATION

Before your group decides to do a fund-raiser, evaluate the idea using this worksheet.

The idea: _____

Purpose: _____

Resources needed: _____

People: _____

Space: _____

Goods: _____

Start-up money: _____

How it benefits the group: _____

How it benefits the person who gives money: _____

Anticipated income: _____

What will be fun about it: _____

The percentage of the proceeds that will be donated to a worthy cause: _____%

Cause to receive the money: _____

Approval for the fund-raiser has been received by:

- ❑ Young people
- ❑ Adults involved
- ❑ Parents
- ❑ Other _____

What has been critical to your fund-raising success in the past? What have been some obstacles? How can you deal with the obstacles? How can you build on your past successes?

---

This page may be reproduced for educational, noncommercial uses only. From *An Asset Builder's Guide to Youth and Money* by Jolene L. Roehlkepartain. Copyright © 1999 by Search Institute, 700 South Third Street, Suite 210, Minneapolis, MN 55415; 800-888-7828; www.search-institute.org.

## Youth Involvement in Grant Making

Philanthropic organizations give money to promote and support the work of individuals or organizations with humanitarian missions. Foundations are the most recognizable form of philanthropic organization. Foundations have a lot of money that they invest, manage, and give away in the form of grants. Grants are sums of money that must be used for a specific purpose.

To give you an idea of what this all means, here is an example: XYC, Inc., is a family-owned company that has made billions of dollars in the packaged foods business. The family member who started the company had an important mentor in her life when she was a teenager. She wanted to make sure that other young people had similar relationships in their own lives, so she started the XYC Foundation in 1985 with a $10 million donation. The foundation invested the $10 million, and the money earned from the investments is given to organizations that work to build mentoring relationships between youth and adults. Staff and board members together make decisions about how to allocate the funds. The organizations that receive the money have to submit proposals telling why their programs are effective and why they need the money, and they have to periodically report back to the foundation on how things are going.

This is an oversimplified example of how foundations work, but it gives you the idea that many important needs are met through this type of funding. Increasingly, young people are getting involved in grant making, especially in helping select recipients for youth-development-focused grants. In some situations, young people are part of the regular decision-making process of the foundation. In other cases, groups of young people receive one large grant from a foundation and divide that into smaller grants within their communities.

Michigan has a particularly progressive approach to youth involvement in grant making. Through a statewide program called the Michigan Community Foundations' Youth Project (MCFYP), young people have been involved in awarding more than $2.3 million to support community projects such as granting a county health department to buy an audiometer to screen children to prevent hearing loss and granting a juvenile court to teach delinquent minors about conflict resolution and cultural diversity.[46]

Youth involvement in grant making is still a relatively new practice, and there can be a lot to learn for a group that is interested in taking it on. But it can also be a great way for young people to have a real and lasting impact on issues they care about.

### Think about It

- What do you know about foundations? What questions do you have about foundations?
- Have you seen foundations contribute to your community or to causes you care about? How?
- Do you know of any groups of young people who have responsibility for giving money away?
- When you've been entrusted with someone else's money or things, how do you feel? How do you responsibly care for those things? How are those experiences similar to what foundations do?
- If you were part of a foundation that gave away money, what would you like to support?
- What's your experience in making group decisions? Do you think it would be easy or difficult to make group decisions about giving money away? Why?
- What connections do you see between an organized youth-led type of giving and your experience in giving money as an individual?

### Try It

- Invite someone from a local community foundation to explain how the organization works. (Identify a person through the local foundation directory at a library, through the yellow pages under "foundations," or through volunteer centers of the United Way.) Ask questions such as these: What needs are met in our community through your foundation? How does your foundation decide which projects to fund? What difference have you seen the funding make?

- Role-play how youth-led grant-making projects operate. Form teams of about four or five people. Tell one of the groups that they have a set amount of money to give away. Tell the rest of the groups that they can try to get some or all of the money by coming up with a creative project that will help the community. Then they will have to convince the group with the funds to support their idea. The group with the funds has to decide how to divide the money between the others.

- Contact a service club (such as Rotary or Lions), a congregation, or a local foundation to ask if they might be able and willing to donate money for your group to actually try out youth-led grant making. As a group, decide on what you want your focus to be and what types of projects you will fund. Then encourage members of your group or other young people to apply for small grants to do small projects such as painting a local community center or holding a book drive for a children's hospital.

- Visit agencies that are recipients of grants. (Contact a local United Way to help you identify organizations that you could visit.) Find out what it's like to receive funds and why it's important. Ask about what kinds of relationships they have with the organizations that give them money.

## Asset Connections

- Youth-led philanthropic projects empower young people by giving them meaningful roles that make a difference in their communities, building asset #7 (community values youth) and asset #8 (youth as resources).

- In working together as a team to award grants, young people need to plan ahead and make decisions (asset #32).

## Did You Know?

The Surdna Foundation established the Student Service and Philanthropy Project in 1991 to set up student-run minifoundations to make grants and learn about philanthropy. Since then, thousands of young people in more than 30 cities and towns across America have participated.[47]

## Organizing People to Help Others

Philanthropy "is the duty of how we should behave when things go wrong for people, and how we can help to make things better for everyone—voluntarily, without being required to do it by the government, and for others, without private gain to ourselves," says Robert L. Payton, professor of philanthropic studies and senior fellow for the Center on Philanthropy. "The history of philanthropy includes the history of efforts to organize people and to mobilize resources to serve public purposes—that is, fund raising."[48]

**WRITE ABOUT IT**

# GRANT REVIEW CHECKLIST

When making group grant-making decisions, it's helpful to follow a grant review process. Use this or a similar process to help you determine how to award grants and to follow up once the grants have been made.

- [ ] 1. Identify the needs of the community or population you are focusing on. For example, if you're targeting young people in grades 9–12, you might want to hold focus groups with people in this age-group to find out about their needs and interests.

- [ ] 2. Publicize that your group is planning to award grants. Create guidelines that help participants know what you expect in terms of a summary of their project. This is known as a request for proposals (RFP).

- [ ] 3. Review proposals individually and rank each with a "1" (for high interest), "2" (for moderate interest), or "3" (low interest).

- [ ] 4. As a group, discuss individual rankings and eliminate proposals that received low-interest ratings from most people.

- [ ] 5. Choose several finalists to interview in person. Ask questions to clarify and get details about their intentions.

- [ ] 6. Work together to identify funding levels according to the needs of each individual proposal, not thinking about the needs of the other proposals.

- [ ] 7. Take votes on whether the group really wants to fund each proposal.

- [ ] 8. Review the accepted proposals and adjust funding levels to fit the total amount you plan to award in grants.

- [ ] 9. Award grants to recipients.

- [ ] 10. Check in regularly with recipients to see how things are going.

- [ ] 11. At the end of each project, assess what went well and what didn't, and what this teaches you about future grant giving.

Once you complete the process of awarding grants for the first time, evaluate your process. What were the strengths? What could be improved? How well did the group work together? What would be helpful to do next time?

This page may be reproduced for educational, noncommercial uses only. From *An Asset Builder's Guide to Youth and Money* by Jolene L. Roehlkepartain. Copyright © 1999 by Search Institute, 700 South Third Street, Suite 210, Minneapolis, MN 55415; 800-888-7828; www.search-institute.org.

Part 2: Core Money Management Issues

## Spending

This final set of money management topics focus on the why most people use their money — by using it to pay for goods or services. People have very different norms around spending and thus there are no hard-and-fast rules about how to make spending decisions. Through discussions of general spending habits, shopping, using credit cards, borrowing, and dealing with debt, this section aims to help you help young people explore their own priorities for spending money, and find strategies that will help them make spending choices they are pleased with.

### Your Spending Habits

Last year, teenagers spent a record $141 billion as a group, which averages out to about $5,420 per teenager. That is twice as much as teens spent 10 years ago.[49]

"Choosing when and what we spend our money on is a lifelong challenge," says Neale S. Godfrey, chairman of the Children's Financial Network.[50] Knowing how to spend money is not something we can check off the list and say, "That's done." New choices, different situations, and changing frames of mind will constantly put us in different places when it comes to our spending decisions.

Learning how to spend money carefully and with forethought isn't easy in an economy and culture that place an incredibly high priority on buying and selling. There are so many choices, and we're bombarded constantly with advertising wherever we go. We receive messages through billboards, mailings, newspapers, magazines, flyers, radio, and television. Those who learn advertising savvy, and make spending choices that are consistent with their plans and goals (which also include saving and giving), are smart consumers. They think before they buy, instead of buying before they think.

There are tools you can use to help you become a smart consumer. But you'll have to do a little thinking and practicing before you find what works best for you.

### Think about It

- What types of things do you spend a lot of money on? Why?
- What types of things do you never or rarely spend money on? Why?
- Have you ever spent more money than you had? When? How often does this happen?
- Who are you most apt to spend money on? Yourself? Your friends? Your family? Why?
- Do you think of yourself as a smart consumer most of the time? Why or why not?

### Try It

- On newsprint, create two columns. Label one "Need" (e.g., things you can't live without, such as food and shelter) and the other one "Want" (e.g., things that aren't basic necessities, such as music CDs and movie tickets). As a group, list things that young people might spend money on and place them under the appropriate category. When you finish, ask questions such as these: Which list is longer? Why do you think that is? How do you decide what is a need and what is a want? How often do you think about this difference when you spend money? Are some people's needs other people's wants? Why or why not? How does this exercise change your attitudes toward spending?
- Ask each individual to determine a personal spending "cooling-off period." One financial expert suggests waiting 30 days between seeing an ad for something you want (but don't absolutely need) and deciding whether or not to spend money on it.[51] Another expert suggests waiting one week for any item that costs $20–$30, two weeks for an item costing $30–$40, and three weeks for an item costing

$40–$50.[52] Ask young people if they think having a cooling-off period is a good idea. Do they agree with the dollar amounts and cooling-off times suggested above? If not, what do they think is reasonable?

- Challenge young people to carry small notebooks with them for one week and to record every time they spend money. Encourage them to include everything: bus rides, gas money, a pack of gum, a snack, an arcade game, a soft drink, a movie, and larger expenses. After a week, bring everyone back together and ask young people to talk about what they learned about their own spending habits and how they felt about keeping track of every penny spent.

## Asset Connections

- Becoming a smart consumer involves having a clear sense of boundaries, which ties into asset #11 (family boundaries) and asset #12 (school boundaries). If young people don't get consistent messages about spending from their families and schools, they might be confused and unsure about how to make good decisions.
- An important aspect of becoming a smart consumer is a new twist on asset #29 (honesty). Young people cannot become smart consumers unless they are honest with themselves about their current and previous spending habits.

## Did You Know?

Shoes and music CDs are some of the most popular items for teenagers to spend money on. But advertisers are finding there are new markets that are capturing teenagers' attention. "Textiles and accessories for the room are two good examples," says Michael Wood, director of syndicated research at Teenage Research Unlimited. "Our research shows that a teenager's room is a domain that they typically have a lot of control over. They make a lot of choices as to how it's decorated and what they and their parents buy for that room." [53]

## Many Spend before They Think

Only 25 percent of mall shoppers go in search of a specific item, say Joe Dominguez and Vicki Robin in *Your Money or Your Life*. Even for adults, 53 percent of groceries and 47 percent of hardware store purchases are made on impulse.[54]

**Part 2: Core Money Management Issues**

### WRITE ABOUT IT

## YOUR SPENDING HISTORY

Spending money is one important way to use money. But too often we view spending with a lot of guilt and a lot of rules — particularly if we've had trouble with overspending in the past or if we feel others think we're not making smart money choices.

Think about your spending history and answer the following questions:

Who supports you the most in your spending decisions? _____

Who thinks you make poor spending choices? _____

What's the most fun you've ever had spending money? _____

What do you most regret spending money on? _____

What's the most money you've ever spent at one time? _____

How did you feel? _____

If you were to grade yourself on your spending history, what grade would you give? Why? _____

What one thing could you change that would improve your spending habits? _____

Do you have personal "rules" about spending? If so, are they helpful, or do they simply cause you to feel guilty about your decisions? What rules could you create that would help you make choices you feel good about?

This page may be reproduced for educational, noncommercial uses only. From *An Asset Builder's Guide to Youth and Money* by Jolene L. Roehlkepartain. Copyright © 1999 by Search Institute, 700 South Third Street, Suite 210, Minneapolis, MN 55415; 800-888-7828; www.search-institute.org.

## Shopping

A 13- to 17-year-old typically takes 15 shopping trips each month.[55] "Kids have never before wielded the purchase power that they wield today," writes Dan Acuff, Ph.D., in *What Kids Buy and Why: The Psychology of Marketing to Kids.*[56] Entire books are now being written on how to appeal to teenage shoppers.

One study of teen spending found that young people average $1,260 per person in income a year. The items young people are most apt to buy include (in order of most likely to be purchased): clothing; away-from-home food (including fast food, groceries, snacks, and candy); video and electronics (such as music CDs and tapes, video rentals, and electronic devices); stationery and school supplies; entertainment (such as movies, sports events, and arcades); personal-care products; sporting goods; toys and games; and reading material. Almost half (48 percent) of what young people bring in gets spent right away, and teenagers set aside about 36 percent of their income for future purchases.[57]

Examining your shopping habits allows you to think about your values, commitments, and future goals. This is important, not only financially, but also personally. People shop for a variety of reasons: to have fun, to meet a need, to purchase a gift, to buy something they want, to kill time, to deal with stress, to see what's new. Shopping is an important part of our American culture, and when people understand how their shopping habits reflect who they are and what they want to do, they make better shopping decisions.

### Think about It

- What do you enjoy shopping for most? Why?
- Who do you enjoy shopping with the most? Why?
- When do you find shopping boring or otherwise unpleasant?
- What's the longest you've waited to buy something that you wanted, to make sure you really wanted it?
- What's your favorite store? Why?
- How often do you buy something impulsively?
- In general, do you think teenagers shop too much, too little, or the right amount? Explain.

### Try It

- With a group of young people, go to a mall or nearby shopping center and visit the stores that appeal to them. Talk about whether or not the stores are appealing to young people in general, and if they are, what makes them so. Are they different from other stores? Notice colors, attitudes of employees toward young people, music, and types of items for sale.
- Challenge teenagers to go on a shopping "fast" or moratorium for one week. Talk about how they feel about that idea. If they will commit to the fast, bring the group back together in one week and talk about how things went.
- Encourage teenagers to examine their shopping habits. Ask questions such as these: How important is shopping to you? Why? How do you feel when you go shopping? How do you feel when you buy things? Have you ever spent too much money? What happened? Have you ever saved money for a long time to buy something special? If so, what? How did you feel? What is your greatest shopping weakness? What is your greatest shopping strength? What would you like to change about your shopping habits? Do you ever buy on impulse? Have you ever experienced buyer's remorse?

### Asset Connections

- When it comes to purchasing decisions, peers have a lot of impact. When buying clothes, teenagers surveyed by BKG Youth say the number one influence is their friends.[58] Young people who make wise purchases are building asset #15 (positive peer influence).

**Part 2: Core Money Management Issues**

- The things young people purchase and the stores they patronize can be a reflection of their level of commitment to asset #27 (equality and social justice). Some young people, for example, refuse to buy clothing made by overworked, underpaid people.

### ❓ Did You Know?

*Zillions,* a magazine for young people from Consumers Union (which also publishes *Consumer Reports*), surveyed 770 9- to 14-year-olds and found that the thing they spend money on the most often is food. Clothes and accessories were next, but only 17 percent said they spent their own money on those things.[59]

### 💲 Buyer's Remorse

Almost 80 of every 100 young people surveyed by *Zillions* magazine said they wished they didn't spend so much money.[60]

### WRITE ABOUT IT

## SHOPPING BY THE MOOD

Pretend that you received $25 as a gift. What would you buy with that money if you were:

In a happy, excited mood? _____

_____

_____

_____

Mad at your parents? _____

_____

_____

_____

Feeling sad and down? _____

_____

_____

_____

Feeling like you owed yourself a big treat? _____

_____

_____

_____

Mad at your best friend? _____

_____

_____

_____

Feeling nervous? _____

_____

_____

_____

Feeling absolutely silly? _____

_____

_____

_____

Some people find that their mood can greatly impact their spending. Others find that their mood doesn't make much difference. Does your mood have an impact on your money decisions? How can you make sound shopping decisions no matter what your mood is?

## Using Credit Cards

Most Americans answer yes to each of these questions about credit card use:

- Do you use at least one credit card on a regular basis?
- Do you write more checks than you used to, even though you use your credit cards, too?
- Do you have at least three credit cards with most of them good at only one particular store or chain of stores?
- Do you think of credit cards primarily as a source of credit and only secondarily as a source of convenience?
- Do you think of credit cards as an evil—a necessary evil, but still an evil—and not a good thing?[61]

"Few Americans tend to think of credit cards as a good thing, whether they use them or not," says Dr. Lewis Mandell, who directed the study that asked the preceding questions. But credit cards themselves are really not a problem. Problems arise when people misuse them. People who think of and record each charge as if it were a cash purchase use credit cards well. Those who pay off their bill each month use credit cards well. Those who have only a few credit cards—ones that they use regularly—use credit cards well. Sylvia Porter points out: "you should not use cards if you're a habitual impulse buyer who frequently buys unnecessary things; if you're habitually late in meeting payments; if you've never managed to live comfortably within your income. And you should certainly shy away if, on top of all these characteristics, you do not have a steady income."[62] A credit card is not a license to overspend but a license to use money well, in a different way than cash or checks.

Because of the temptation to misuse credit cards, some people choose to live credit card free. Others use credit cards but keep the balance limits low as a way of not overusing them. (You can call credit companies at any time and ask to have your limit lowered.)

Other people find credit cards can help them with major purchases on a more timely basis (such as making travel arrangements over the phone, renting cars, or buying concert tickets). In addition, some credit cards offer perks and bonuses. For example, airlines have credit cards that earn frequent-flyer miles; other companies (such as car companies and video stores) allow users to earn store credits that can be used to purchase items at that specific store or company. While these perks can be nice, keep in mind that credit card companies are in the business because they make a lot of money on the interest and fees that they charge.

So, there are benefits to having credit cards and there are reasons to be wary of them. If you are considering getting a credit card or already have one, you need to learn how to manage them if you are going to live wisely and responsibly and be financial healthy.

### Think about It

- Do you have a credit card? Why or why not?
- What have you learned about credit cards from your family?
- How would you answer the five questions in the introduction to this section? How would your parent(s) or guardian(s)? How would other family members?
- Is there an ideal age for a person to get her or his first credit card? What is it? Why?
- Do you think credit cards are a good idea?

### Try It

- Visit a store that young people enjoy. Have each young person bring a pad of paper and pen to write down everything they would buy if they had a credit card. At the end of the trip, talk about young people's lists. Ask them how the lists would differ if they had a $20 or $50 bill instead. Talk about differences in how they approach spending depending upon whether they have a credit card or cash.

- Give young people math problems that relate to credit cards. For example, if you had a $100 balance on your credit card, and you could only make the minimum monthly payments of $25, how many months would it take you to pay off your balance at a 15 percent interest rate? And how much interest would you end up paying?[63]

- Have young people research the differences between the Discover card, the American Express card, and a Visa or MasterCard.[64] Ask them to compare interest rates, annual fees, and award programs, if any.

### Asset Connections

- Using a credit card well requires planning and decision making (asset #32). A lot of people use a credit card without thinking. Those who plan ahead and think about the choices they're making when they use credit cards, often use them more wisely.

### Did You Know?

The largest collection of valid, usable credit cards belongs to Walter Cavanagh of Santa Clara, California. He has 1,397 cards in a 250-foot-long wallet that weighs 38 pounds 8 ounces. If Cavanagh decided to max out all of his cards one day, he could rack up a $1.65 million debt.[65]

### Bankruptcy and Credit Card Debt

In a study of people filing for personal bankruptcy, researchers found that these debtors earned an average of $19,800 a year and had an average credit card debt of $17,544.[66]

### WRITE ABOUT IT

## YOUR CREDIT CARDS

How many credit cards do you have now? How many do you expect to have in the future? Which ones do you think you'll probably have? In the space below, draw an outline of each credit card you expect to have in your lifetime and label each according to who issues it (such as Visa, MasterCard, Discover, American Express, a department store, or a gas station).

How does the number of cards you expect to have in your life compare to the number that your parent(s) or guardian(s) have? Do you think it's better to have a lot of credit cards to choose from, just one or two, or none at all? Why?

## Borrowing

Generally, people borrow money when they want or need to buy something and they don't have the cash to pay for it. In addition to using credit cards, ways of borrowing include taking out a loan from a bank, getting an advance on a paycheck, or asking your family or friends for some cash until you can pay them back. While it's probably the cheapest and easiest way to borrow, getting money from family and friends can also lead to trouble.

Most often when a friend or family member lends you money, you pay it back when you can without interest or a payment plan. That's when the trouble starts, because borrowing means living beyond your means (spending more than you have), and if there are no restrictions on it, it can get to be a habit. In addition, borrowing from individuals, without an agreement about paying it back, can cause tension in the relationship.

Using credit cards as a way of borrowing has its own potential for problems. Every time you use a credit card to pay for something and you don't pay off the monthly balance, you are charged interest (a certain percentage of your balance that is added to your total amount owed). The rates that credit card companies charge are usually very high compared with what you would pay for a loan from a bank. And, each time you are charged interest that you can't pay off, you add to your balance, which increases the interest you are charged in the future.

It's important to have clear boundaries for yourself about when it's appropriate to borrow money and when it's not. People who borrow money all the time to get the things they want are doing themselves a disservice. On the other hand, people can develop important money management skills when they borrow money periodically, make a commitment to the lender about when they'll pay them back, and negotiate the amount of interest they'll pay, especially if they're borrowing a large amount of money.

### Think about It

- How is borrowing money the same as borrowing an item, such as a jacket? How is it different?
- What have your parent(s) or guardian(s) borrowed money to pay for? (Possibilities include cars, homes, education, travel, gifts, and medical and dental expenses.)
- What would you borrow money for? What would you never borrow money for?
- How often do you borrow money? Why?
- Has anyone ever borrowed money from you? What was that like?
- When you borrow money from someone, should that person have a say in how you use it? Should you have a say when you lend money to someone?
- Do you think your borrowing money is within normal money management boundaries? Why or why not?

### Try It

- Give all but three people three rubber bands (or another object). Give the remaining three people 10 rubber bands each. Say something like: "By the end of this activity, anyone who has seven or more rubber bands can use them to buy [choose a privilege or reward]. Those of you with three rubber bands will have to figure out how to convince the people who have 10 to lend or give you some of theirs." Give young people time to do this activity. Stop when it seems like most people have at least seven. Some young people will have seven or more rubber bands, others probably won't (depending on the number of people in your group, it is possible that each person will end up with seven). Ask questions such as these: How difficult was it to get rubber bands? Why? Who had the most power? What kinds of things did you have to do or say to get more rubber bands? How did it feel to have a lot of rubber bands and to have people trying to get them from you? How did you feel when I said that time was up? Does this activity tell you anything about borrowing? How do you feel about some people not being able to afford the reward? Give everyone a reward for participating.

- Lend each young person money (an amount you wouldn't mind losing). Or single out a few young people and give them money. Tell them that they can do what they want with it, but that you want it back in one week. Don't talk about the money once you've distributed it. After one week, bring the group back together and ask for your money. See who remembered to return it. Find out what people did with it during the week. (Some may have spent it, others may have saved it in a jar, and some may even have put it in a bank.) Talk about the responsibility that people who borrow have to return the money on time. Discuss whether they also have a responsibility to use the borrowed money in certain ways.

- Encourage young people to interview a person they've borrowed money from in the past, asking questions such as these: How did you feel about lending me money when I initially asked? How did you feel after I had paid you back? Do you feel I paid you back in an adequate amount of time? Why or why not? Would you lend me money in the future? Why or why not? If young people have never borrowed money before, encourage them to interview someone whom they would consider asking to borrow money from.

## Asset Connections

- Borrowing money can give a young person a sense of personal power (asset #37) as long as there are appropriate expectations regarding how and when the money will be repaid.
- Borrowing is most effective when lenders have high expectations (asset #16) regarding young people's responsibility (asset #30).

## Did You Know?

The number one reason American adults borrow money is to buy a house. Here's what people who borrow money say they spend it on:

   To buy a home     65.2%
   To invest in real estate    15.3%
   To buy a car     7.1%
   To pay for goods and services    5.2%
   To pay for an education    2.5%
   Other miscellaneous loans    2.0%
   Home improvement projects    1.9%
   To make investments, other than
       real estate    0.9%[67]

## The Interest Rate for Family Borrowing

Financial expert and author Jean Ross Peterson suggests that young people who borrow money from family members should have an interest rate of five cents for every dollar borrowed.[68]

**WRITE ABOUT IT**

# WHERE YOU BORROW MONEY FROM

Use this quiz to help you think about your borrowing habits or intentions.

Have you ever borrowed money before?   ❑ Yes   ❑ No

If so, how often do you borrow money? _____

_____

Whom have you borrowed money from? Check all that apply.

❑ Your parent(s) or guardian(s)

❑ Your friends

❑ A bank

❑ A credit card company (each time you don't pay off your monthly balance in full or you pay it late, you're borrowing money)

❑ Your employer (such as asking for an advance)

❑ Another relative

❑ A pawnshop

❑ Other (specify): _____

Whom would you consider borrowing money from? Check all that apply.

❑ Your parent(s) or guardian(s)

❑ Your friends

❑ Your credit card company

❑ Your employer

❑ Another relative

❑ A pawnshop

❑ A bank

❑ Other (specify): _____

If you've ever borrowed money, were you charged interest?

❑ Yes. How much? _____

❑ No.

How do you feel about being charged interest for borrowing money? How do you feel about your current borrowing situation? Do you consider yourself experienced in borrowing? Why or why not? What do you think you might borrow to pay for in the future?

---

This page may be reproduced for educational, noncommercial uses only. From *An Asset Builder's Guide to Youth and Money* by Jolene L. Roehlkepartain. Copyright © 1999 by Search Institute, 700 South Third Street, Suite 210, Minneapolis, MN 55415; 800-888-7828; www.search-institute.org.

## Part 2: Core Money Management Issues

### Dealing with Debt

Any time you borrow money, no matter how insignificant it may seem, you are going into debt. For some people, debt is not a problem — they accept borrowing as a way to pay for things they couldn't otherwise afford, and they have a plan for how they will pay it back. On the other hand, staying out of debt is important to some people for personal or cultural reasons. And, for many people debt becomes a major issue because they don't have the resources to pay it back, so they get into a cycle that draws them even further into debt.

Debt becomes a problem when people regularly live beyond their means or get hit with an unexpected financial crisis. Finding a balance between having money in savings in case of emergencies and paying off debts can also become difficult. "The best way to manage your personal debt is to borrow only for appropriate reasons and to pay off all loans within a reasonable period of time," says financial expert Jonathan Pond. "Good debt finances something worthwhile that will benefit you well into the future. Bad debt usually finances something that you use up almost immediately or from which you never receive any real benefit."[69]

Dealing with debt is part of our capitalist society today. In the 1950s and 1960s, young people starting out could often do so without going into debt. Credit cards as we know them didn't exist then, and loans weren't as common as they are today. People who make financial plans and goals will find that there are sometimes good reasons to take on debt, and even those who have strong financial planning skills will find at times that they want or need things they don't have the money to pay for. Knowing how to manage debt can be key to making plans for the future.

### Think about It

- Do you think going into debt is a problem in our society? Why or why not?
- What stories have you heard about people dealing with debt? How do these stories make you feel?
- What do members of your family think about debt? If you're not sure, ask them.
- Do you have cultural norms regarding debt? What are they? Do you know their history?
- There are positive, worthwhile reasons that people go into debt? What are they?
- If you found yourself in debt and didn't know how you could repay it, what would you do? Why?

### Try It

- Invite someone from a bank or credit union to speak to your group about debt counseling. Brainstorm a list of questions to ask, such as: When do people usually come in for debt counseling? How long does it typically take for people to get out of debt trouble? What do you wish people knew about money management to avoid getting into too much debt? What's your opinion about debt in this country, particularly since most people need to take on some debt at some point in their lives?
- Form three groups of approximately the same number of young people. Assign each group one of these categories: post–high school education, gift for someone you really care about, car. Have each group discuss the following questions with the category it has been assigned. Is this something worth going into debt over? Why or why not? If you were to go into debt for this item, what's the maximum dollar amount you'd spend? Why? What's the longest loan repayment that you'd take on (for example, home mortgages typically are 15-, 20-, and 30-year loans)? Why?

## Asset Connections

- When young people find themselves in debt, it's helpful if they can seek advice and counsel from a parent or guardian (asset #2: positive family communication) or from another caring adult (asset #3). Dealing with debt is difficult to do alone, and help from others can be critical for finding a solution to the situation.

## Did You Know?

A lot of Americans find themselves pushing their financial boundaries to the point of needing help. Each year 1.13 million Americans file for personal bankruptcy protection.[70]

## How Much Is Too Much?

"If more than 15 percent of your net income goes to pay debt, then you're looking at a danger level," says Jonathan Pond. "When you're paying off money you borrowed at that rate, it will be much more difficult to save money."[71]

## WRITE ABOUT IT

# WHAT WOULD YOU GO INTO DEBT FOR?

Listed below are 10 items that some people go into debt to pay for. Prioritize this list on a scale from 1 (meaning most likely to go into debt for) to 10 (least likely to go into debt for).

_____ Basic needs such as food and shelter for your family

_____ A house

_____ A car

_____ Post–high school education

_____ A necessary home repair that pops up

_____ To start a business

_____ An important surgery not fully covered by insurance

_____ A vacation

_____ Throwing a big party for all of your friends

_____ Buying a gift for someone you really care about

Are there other things that you'd be willing to go into debt to pay for? What are they? Is there a limit to how much you would borrow to pay for each of these?

_____
_____
_____
_____
_____
_____
_____
_____
_____
_____
_____
_____
_____
_____
_____
_____

This page may be reproduced for educational, noncommercial uses only. From *An Asset Builder's Guide to Youth and Money* by Jolene L. Roehlkepartain. Copyright © 1999 by Search Institute, 700 South Third Street, Suite 210, Minneapolis, MN 55415; 800-888-7828; www.search-institute.org.

# PART 3
# WHAT OTHERS CAN DO TO TEACH AND MODEL FINANCIAL RESPONSIBILITY

Young people need positive experiences and stimulating relationships to become caring, competent adults. As young people work toward financial health, they need the support and encouragement, as well as the positive example, of people around them.

Families, schools, youth-serving organizations, and congregations have critical roles in the positive development of young people. In this section are four reproducible handouts that give practical ideas on how individuals and organizations can foster the healthy development of young people and build their financial skills. These handouts discuss:

- How Families Can Model and Teach Financial Responsibility
- How Schools Can Model and Teach Financial Responsibility
- How Youth-Serving Organizations Can Model and Teach Financial Responsibility
- How Congregations Can Model and Teach Financial Responsibility

Use these handouts often. Distribute them while you're using this guide with your young people or provide them during financial workshops or seminars that you give. Make as many copies as you wish and give them to as many people as you want. Spread the word about the importance of building the financial skills of young people as you encourage the development of young people to their full potential.

# HOW FAMILIES CAN MODEL AND TEACH FINANCIAL RESPONSIBILITY

The number one thing teenagers want to talk more about with their parents is the family finances, according to a Gallup study.* Family support is important for young people in money matters. In fact, many teenagers say their parents' support of their purchases matters a lot to them. Sixty-three percent of teenagers surveyed by Market Facts Inc. said, "What my parents think about the things I buy is very important to me."** Families, especially parents and guardians, have a great deal of influence on the money choices their teenagers make, even if it doesn't seem like it. It's important for families to be open about financial matters and teach and model for young people the financial skills they need. Here are some ideas for building financial skills in young people:

## Financial Plans and Goals

▶ Help your teenager set up a budget that realistically reflects her or his income and expenses. Share your experiences with budgeting.

▶ Talk with your teenager about the money messages he or she gets in different settings: at school, with friends, in your congregation, from the media, and within your family. Discuss the consistency or inconsistency of these messages and how to make sense of all that in light of your teenager's financial and life plans and goals.

## Income

▶ Consider giving your teenager an allowance (if you don't already do so) or find some projects around your home for which your teenager can earn money. Young people need income to practice using money wisely.

▶ As teenagers become older, give them more financial responsibility. For example, instead of buying their clothes, consider giving them a regular clothing allowance and responsibility for doing their own shopping.

▶ When your teenager wants to borrow money from you, charge interest and agree to a payment plan. Talk about the number of payments and the amount that needs to be paid back each time. Even if a teenager is borrowing only $20, having a formal agreement can help prepare her or him for loans later in life.

## Saving

▶ Once a year, bring family members together to set individual and family saving goals. Throughout the year, check on the progress of each person. A year later, challenge everyone to save a little bit more.

▶ Assist your teenager in opening up a savings account at a bank if he or she hasn't already done so. If your teenager already has a savings account, encourage her or him either to make deposits more regularly or to save a little more.

## Giving

▶ Encourage each family member to give a certain percentage of her or his money to worthy causes during the year. Be a role model for giving.

▶ Include your teenager in family decisions about how much to give and to whom.

▶ Talk with your children about issues that are important to them. Help them find groups or organizations to give money to that are working on these issues.

▶ Talk about your values regarding caring for and helping other people.

## Spending

▶ Go shopping with your teenager. Model responsible spending and talk with your teenager about how you make shopping decisions.

▶ Allow your teenager to learn from overspending, and expect teenagers to do this a number of times as they learn about spending. Figure out ways for teenagers to personally experience the consequences of overspending (for example, having to pay interest on unpaid credit card balances).

▶ Be open about your family's spending habits, particularly during times when money is tight and spending needs to be cut back or closely controlled. Being honest about these situations helps young people learn how to deal with overspending when it happens.

---

* George Gallup Jr., "Teens Want a Better Understanding of the Family Finances," *Gallup Youth Survey*, September 25, 1985.

** James Green, Marie Drum Beninati, and Steven Jacober, *Capturing the Purchasing Power of Kids: A Guide to Kids' Interaction at Retail* (Tucson, AZ: Lisa Frank, 1994), 8.

Part 3: What Others Can Do to Teach and Model Financial Responsibility

# HOW SCHOOLS CAN MODEL AND TEACH FINANCIAL RESPONSIBILITY

Schools have tremendous potential for teaching young people financial skills in the context of their overall education. For many young people, particularly those who move around a lot, school is the only formal institution they're connected to. In addition, the nature of education lends itself well to include the teaching of money management. Here are some ideas for building financial skills in young people:

## Financial Plans and Goals

▶ When doing class projects that involve money (such as fund-raisers or service projects), have young people complete budgets and create the financial plans.

▶ Teach young people about making financial plans and goals in the context of helping them sort through the messages they hear about money. For example, talk about common money-related phrases, such as "Money doesn't grow on trees," "It's just a waste of money," and "Money can't buy love." Discuss how these and other messages about money affect the way young people make financial plans and goals.

## Income

▶ Give young people an opportunity to showcase their talents, see what others can do, and think about how they can use those skills and interests to make money. One way to do this is to have an entrepreneurs fair where participants design businesses or services they think they could offer. This type of fair isn't intended to generate income for young people, but rather to get them thinking creatively about the possibilities they could explore.

▶ Don't exclude any student from an activity because he or she can't afford to pay for it. If you offer opportunities that need to be funded beyond your school's budget, make sure that you build in ways for young people to get scholarships or do work-study in order to cover the costs. This policy should include in-school activities like field trips and special events, as well as cocurricular things like theater, debate, and sports teams.

## Saving

▶ Partner with a local bank to offer an evening workshop at your school for students and their families to talk about student saving accounts. Many families may not be comfortable dealing with banks or have easy access to them during banking hours.

▶ Encourage young people to set short- and long-term savings goals. Discuss their progress along the way and set up systems to celebrate and recognize their achievements when they reach their goals.

## Giving

▶ Use at least one fund-raiser a year as a way to generate money to donate to a cause your students care about. Make sure students research different organizations well before making choices about where to give.

▶ Invite someone from an educational charity (or someone from your school district's nonprofit arm if it has one) to talk about these types of charities and why they're important.

## Spending

▶ Create cafeteria debit cards for students to buy so that they don't need to carry cash every day and so that they can become proficient in using "plastic" in responsible ways. You could offer debit cards with different values, such as $10 and $20.

▶ Put young people in charge of disbursing school supplies to classrooms at the beginning of the school year. (Have teachers create their shopping lists of supplies based on their needs and budgets.) Although money won't change hands, this system gives young people experience in handling teachers' shopping lists, budgets, and coordinating all the requests and fulfilling them.

---

This page may be reproduced for educational, noncommercial uses only. From *An Asset Builder's Guide to Youth and Money* by Jolene L. Roehlkepartain. Copyright © 1999 by Search Institute, 700 South Third Street, Suite 210, Minneapolis, MN 55415; 800-888-7828; www.search-institute.org.

# HOW YOUTH-SERVING ORGANIZATIONS CAN MODEL AND TEACH FINANCIAL RESPONSIBILITY

For young people to succeed, they need the financial skills to back up their personal goals, dreams, and hopes. Bring out the best in young people by providing not only programs that enhance their general skills and interests but also ones that teach money management. Here are some ideas for building financial skills in young people:

## Financial Plans and Goals

▶ Have a youth treasurer who is involved in budgeting and planning in your organization or for specific programs or events.

▶ Enrich your setting with posters and quotes that emphasize money management and financial goals. Use these in your programming to spark conversations about money issues.

## Income

▶ Develop a system for young people to launch their own businesses under the auspices of your organization. For example, teen entrepreneurs in Washington, D.C., developed Transforming Futures. This business works with Spanish-speaking parents and their children by providing bilingual workbooks and audiotapes to build English proficiency while preserving individuals' Spanish skills.*

▶ If your programming requires youth to pay for their involvement, find as many ways as possible to offer scholarships, work programs, and other ways of helping young people fund their involvement. Don't forget about hidden costs as well such as T-shirts, special events, or supplies.

---

* "Venture Capital: Teen-Powered Enterprises ID Local Needs and Fill Them," *Assets: The Magazine of Ideas for Healthy Communities and Healthy Youth,* Summer 1998, 3.

## Saving

▶ Teach young people about how programs can save money when they use resources wisely and partner with other organizations. For example, if young people want to plan an event that requires a larger facility than what you have, encourage them to explore the costs of renting a facility in addition to seeing how they could barter or have space donated by another youth-serving organization.

▶ Offer an investment club for teenagers (either as role-playing or for investing small amounts of money) so that young people can learn about this form of long-term savings while also experiencing a supportive group that's interested in talking about money issues.

## Giving

▶ Team up with a philanthropic organization in your community to provide a workshop on giving.

▶ Offer service projects that encourage young people to give not only of their time but also of their money. (Be sensitive to the different income levels of your young people.) For example, young people could give part of their allowance or raise money by doing some odd jobs to buy a holiday present for a child while your group has a toy drive that encourages others to donate toys as well.

## Spending

▶ Develop strategies for actively involving parents in programs that teach positive spending habits. Encourage open communication, humor, and practical skills that empower both parents and young people.

▶ Publish a list of free and inexpensive ideas for things that teenagers can do with their families in your community. Emphasize the importance of spending time — not just money — to build family relationships.

# HOW CONGREGATIONS CAN MODEL AND TEACH FINANCIAL RESPONSIBILITY

Congregations of all faiths are in the unique position of not only nurturing young people's spiritual development but also having opportunities to help young people to examine their values in general and specifically in the area of money management. Many people in a congregation can play roles in modeling and teaching young people financial skills in terms of making ethical, generous, and responsible choices. Here are some ideas for building financial skills in young people:

## Financial Plans and Goals

▶ Help young people develop personal purpose statements that reflect who they are and what they want to do in accordance with their values, commitments, and priorities. Afterward, talk with them about how these statements impact their financial plans and goals.

▶ Offer a financial values workshop for young people to help them understand how identifying personal values is critical for making meaningful personal financial goals.

## Income

▶ Provide opportunities for young people to meet and talk with adults who have jobs that directly reflect their values and priorities, not just their interest in earning money.

▶ Be creative in the ways you ask young people to raise income for your programming. Involve them in selecting ways to raise income in addition to participating in the process of doing so.

## Saving

▶ Talk with young people about your tradition's sacred writings regarding using money wisely. Explore together how these messages relate to saving.

▶ Present a workshop on social-investment funds that have guidelines that fit with your faith tradition. Talk about how young people can make investments that are consistent with their values and beliefs.

## Giving

▶ Let young people choose group fund-raisers that address needs in your community, country, and world. Involve them in the planning, leading, and carrying out of all aspects of fund-raising efforts, particularly the financial parts.

▶ Invite adults in your congregation who enjoy giving money to talk to teenagers about their experiences and interest in giving.

▶ Annually fund (by making it part of your congregational budget) a youth philanthropic committee. Have young people set guidelines for giving and evaluate applications before making decisions on disbursing the funds.

▶ Discuss how giving is taught in your sacred writings.

## Spending

▶ Allow young people to analyze and critique the congregation's budget in regards to its spending. Talk about young people's views on what the expense items say about the congregation's priorities, traditions, and values.

▶ Create a congregational-wide shopping fair during holiday times. Have members of all ages (children, youth, and adults) make items to sell. This gives young people the chance to shop for items that support their congregation and its members.

This page may be reproduced for educational, noncommercial uses only. From *An Asset Builder's Guide to Youth and Money* by Jolene L. Roehlkepartain. Copyright © 1999 by Search Institute, 700 South Third Street, Suite 210, Minneapolis, MN 55415; 800-888-7828; www.search-institute.org.

# RECOMMENDED RESOURCES

## TEENAGERS AND FINANCIAL MANAGEMENT

*It Doesn't Grow on Trees* by Jean Ross Peterson (White Hall, VA: Betterway Publications, 1988). This book combines practical information with humor on how to raise financially independent and responsible young people.

*Money Doesn't Grow on Trees: A Parent's Guide to Raising Financially Responsible Children* by Neale S. Godfrey (New York: Fireside, Simon & Schuster 1994). In this *New York Times* best-seller, Godfrey gives the basics about money so that young people can learn to use it effectively and responsibly.

*Our Vulnerable Youth: The Financial Literacy of American 12th Graders* by Lewis Mandell, Ph.D. (Washington, DC: Jump$tart Coalition for Personal Financial Literacy, 1998). This report presents the results of a multiple-choice exam taken by 1,532 high school seniors throughout the United States to test their basic financial skills.

*A Penny Saved: Teaching Your Children the Values and Life Skills They Will Need to Live in the Real World* by Neale S. Godfrey (New York: Simon & Schuster, 1995). Through games and exercises, this book shows parents how to instill values and life skills through teaching money management skills to young people.

*Student Service and Philanthropy Project* developed by the Surdna Foundation and the New York City Board of Education Division of High Schools (New York: Surdna Foundation, 1994). This in-depth guide gives practical ways to establish and operate a youth-run philanthropic foundation.

*Volunteering and Giving among Teenagers 12 to 17 Years of Age* by the Independent Sector (Washington, DC: Independent Sector, 1997). This 126-page report presents findings on a study of young people's giving and volunteer habits.

*What Kids Buy and Why: The Psychology of Marketing to Kids* by Dan Acuff, Ph.D. (New York: Free Press, 1997). Written for those interested in marketing products and services to young people, this book explains what appeals to young people of different ages—and why.

*When Teenagers Work* by Ellen Greenberger and Laurence Steinberg (New York: Basic Books, 1986). This provocative book, based on the current research about teenagers who have part- or full-time jobs, highlights how to make the most out of teenage work experiences.

*Youth as Philanthropist Developing Habits of the Heart* by the Community Partnerships with Youth Inc. (Fort Wayne, IN: Community Partnerships with Youth Inc., 1999). This manual teaches the traditions of philanthropy and suggests ways for young people to develop the skills, commitments, and values to become generous people.

## GENERAL BOOKS ABOUT FINANCIAL MANAGEMENT

*The Complete Guide to Managing Your Money* by Janet Bamford, Jeff Blyskal, Emily Card, and Aileen Jacobson (Mount Vernon, NY: Consumers Union, 1989). Published by Consumer Reports Books, this book gives comprehensive information on money management based on the knowledge and research of numerous financial experts.

*Courage to Be Rich: Creating a Life of Spiritual and Material Abundance* by Suze Orman (New York: Riverhead/Putnam, 1999). This book explores the psychological, moral, and ethical aspects of personal finance while guiding readers in how to create a rich life that uses their talents, interests, and skills to their full potential.

*How to Turn Your Money Life Around* by Ruth Hayden (Deerfield Beach, FL: Health Communications, Inc., 1992). Written for women, this book shows how to make money a positive force in everyday life.

*Money Savvy: How to Live Rich on Any Income* edited by Stephen C. George (Emmaus, PA: Rodale Press, 1998). This practical guide gives helpful, easy-to-understand information on the various aspects of money management.

*The New Century Family Money Book* by Jonathan Pond (New York: Dell, 1993). This comprehensive guide gives a complete picture on total money management from taxes to health costs to spending and saving.

*The 9 Steps to Financial Freedom* by Suze Orman (New York: Crown, 1997). This book outlines the philosophical and spiritual aspects of creating a life that allows you to be who you want to be without the constraints of financial worries.

*1001 Ways to Cut Your Expenses* by Jonathan D. Pond (New York: Dell, 1992). When money gets tight, this book lists 1001 cost-cutting tips that help you gain control of your finances.

*Your Money or Your Life* by Joe Dominguez and Vicki Robin (New York: Penguin, 1992). This book explores ways to transform your relationship with money so that you can do the work you really want to do and live in ways that you've always dreamed of.

## WEB SITES ABOUT TEENAGERS AND FINANCIAL MANAGEMENT

http://www.investorguide.com/Kids.htm. An interactive site that teaches young people about investing.

http://www.kiplinger.com. Features 11 departments about money management, from spending to insurance to stocks. It also has a department called "Kids and Money."

http://pages.prodigy.com/kidsmoney/. Has surveys for young people to take about their money use along with information from other surveys.

http://www.give.org. Promotes well-informed giving by providing information collected by the National Charities Information Bureau.

http://www.indepsec.org. Provides access to extensive research on the giving habits of American adults and youth.

http://www.msu.edu/~k12phil/. Outlines curricula and tools that teach young people about the nonprofit sector in American society.

http://www.mcfyp.org. Highlights the work of young people involved in youth advisory committees that award grants in the state of Michigan.

http://www.ncfe.org. A site by the nonprofit organization National Center for Finance Education that is dedicated to helping people learn to manage money.

http://www.kidsmoneystore.com. Lists hundreds of resources (from books to board games) for young people to learn about money.

http://www.jumpstartcoalition.org/welcome.html. Emphasizes the financial skills young people need to know about money before they graduate from high school.

http://www.inswebpro.com/carriers/nefe. Includes articles on personal finance, information about the National Endowment for Financial Education's program on personal finance, and hands-on financial planning materials.

http://www.girlsinc.org. Focuses on what girls need to succeed by including research and tips for raising financially savvy girls.

## FINANCIAL SOFTWARE PACKAGES

Quicken is one of the most popular, inexpensive, and easy-to-use financial software packages that allows people to track their banking, investing, debts, and assets while creating budgets and financial plans. Many people use it to create some what-if scenarios, such as buying a certain stock or mutual fund.

Quicken has more of the accounting features needed for those who run their own business. It can create invoices, paychecks, and numerous financial reports.

# GLOSSARY

**Advance:** Payment of money before it is due. Getting an advance on your paycheck means that you receive the check before you have completed the work.

**Automated teller machine (ATM):** A computerized terminal at which customers can perform a variety of banking transactions, such as make deposits or withdrawals, 24 hours a day.

**Automatic investing:** Investing money on a regular basis (such as monthly or quarterly) through an automatic transfer from another type of account (such as savings or checking).

**Balance:** The amount of money in a bank or other financial account.

**Bankruptcy:** A legal process by which a person declares that he or she doesn't have enough money to pay all that he or she owes. Control of the person's finances is turned over to a court to distribute any remaining money to those who are owed.

**Bond:** An "I owe you" statement that companies or the government sell to the general public to raise money.

**Bounced check:** A check that the bank refuses ("bounces back") because there is not enough money in your account to cover the check.

**Budget:** A plan that shows how much money you have, how much you earn, how you plan to use it, and how you actually use it.

**Capitalism:** Economic system practiced in the United State and other Western countries, which allows the individual ownership of land, buildings, and equipment. Distribution of resources is controlled by competition in a free market.

**Capitalist:** A person who supports the system of capitalism.

**Certificate of deposit (CD):** A type of investment in which money is deposited for a specific amount of time (such as six months) at a specific rate of interest.

**Closing price:** The price of an investment at the end of the trading day.

**Credit card:** A card that allows people to make purchases by loans.

**Credit card debt:** The amount of money owed to a credit card company.

**Credit union:** A financial institution that provides banking services to certain groups of people with something in common, such as people who work for the same company or are in the same profession.

**Debt:** Something, often money, owed to someone else, with an obligation to pay her or him back.

**Debt counseling:** The process of receiving advice on how to get out of debt.

**Debtor:** One who owes something to another.

**Dollar-cost averaging:** The average cost per share, figured annually, on an investment that has been purchased on a regular basis (such as monthly or quarterly).

**Entrepreneur:** One who manages, owns, or creates a business.

**Estate:** All of the possessions a person owns. Usually referred to when speaking of the money and property owned and debts owed by a person who has died.

**Expenditure:** Money spent.

**Expenses:** Specific amounts that are required to be paid in order to reach a certain goal. Could be thought of as the price of achieving that certain goal. For example, gas and repairs are some of the expenses of owning a car.

**Financial reserves:** A certain amount of money set aside for a special purpose or future use.

**Fund:** Another name for a mutual fund.

**Fund-raising:** Soliciting money from others to give to an organization or campaign or to accomplish a specific goal. For example, to finance a trip to Europe a school club holds a fund-raising dinner at which proceeds from the sale of the dinner tickets go toward the cost of the trip.

**Grant:** Money that is given, after certain requirements are met, from one to another for a specific purpose or goal. For example, some college students receive grants from the government to help pay for the cost of their schooling.

**Income:** Money a person receives that can be spent. Income might come from a job, allowance, or gift.

**Income source:** The person or place that supplies income. An income source may be your parents, who supply your allowance, or your boss, who pays you wages.

**Interest:** The charge for borrowing money. You may receive interest from a bank when you put money in an account, because the bank borrows your money and lends it to other people. Those other people pay for borrowing money from the bank. It is also the monthly fee you pay on a loan or credit card.

**Investments:** An enterprise people put money into with the goal of getting even more money back.

**Investor:** A person who buys stocks, bonds, or mutual funds.

**Loan:** Money that is given to another that has to be paid back. A loan is most often given for a specific amount of time and usually has to be paid back with interest.

**Loan repayment:** The process of having to pay back money that was borrowed. Usually done as a series of regular payments made over a predetermined amount of time.

**Means:** The amount of wealth or property a person has. If a person has the means to buy a house, he or she has the money to make the purchase.

**Mortgage:** A loan from a bank or other financial institution used to buy a house or other piece of property.

**Mutual fund:** A mixture of investments that represent a number of different companies and/or types of businesses.

**Net spendable income:** The amount of money that is left over after required expenses such as groceries, house payment, and car payment. Your net spendable income would be the amount that you could use to spend on entertainment or clothing because you have already paid your required expenses.

**Net worth:** The total amount remaining after all expenses and debts have been paid. If you have $1,000 in the bank and you own a car that is worth $2,000 and you have a house that is worth $60,000 but on which you owe $30,000, you can figure your net worth by adding everything you own and subtracting what you owe. In this example, your net worth would be $33,000.

**Overdraft fees:** Fees a bank charges if you write a check for an amount that is more than the amount you have in your account.

**Philanthropist:** A person who actively promotes the well-being of others through donations of time and/or money.

**Price per share:** The price of a single stock or mutual fund share.

**Proceeds:** The amount of money that is obtained

## Glossary

either from a fund-raiser or after something is sold. The amount of money you gathered from your garage sale would be considered your proceeds.

**Return:** In terms of an investment, the amount of money that one receives from making the investment.

**Royalties:** A portion paid to an author out of the profits resulting from the sale of her or his work.

**Savings:** Money set aside to be used at a later date.

**Share:** A unit of ownership of the stock of a company.

**Social-investment funds:** Mutual funds that do not invest in companies that manufacture or sell certain types of products (such as weapons or tobacco) or engage in certain practices (such as animal testing or violating human rights).

**Stock:** A part or share of a company that the general public can purchase; also known as a share or shares.

**Stock market:** An institution where shares of many companies are bought and sold.

**Tax-deductible donation:** An amount, established by the government, that can be subtracted from the taxes you owe for donating a specific item. If you give some clothing to Goodwill this is considered a tax-deductible donation and the value of the donation can be subtracted from your total taxable income.

Definitions adapted from *Merriam-Webster's Collegiate Dictionary*, 10th ed. (Springfield, MA: Merriam-Webster, Inc., 1997); Steve Otfinoski, *The Kid's Guide to Money: Earning It, Saving It, Spending It, Growing It, Sharing It* (New York: Scholastic, 1996); and www.girlsinc.org.

# NOTES

### INTRODUCTION

[1] Constance Casey, "Success Story: Author Michener Found Joy Giving Away Fortune," *Minneapolis Star Tribune,* November 8, 1997, 6.

### PART 1: THE ASSET APPROACH TO FINANCIAL RESPONSIBILITY

[2] Steve Farkas and Jean Johnson, with Ann Duffett and Ali Bers, *Kids These Days: What Americans Really Think about the Next Generation* (New York: Public Agenda, 1997), 46.

[3] Lloyd D. Johnston, Jerald G. Bachman, and Patrick M. O'Malley, *Monitoring the Future: Questionnaire Responses from the Nation's High School Seniors, 1995* (Ann Arbor: Institute for Social Research, University of Michigan, 1997), 166.

[4] Guinness Media Inc., *The Guinness Book of World Records: 1998* (New York: Bantam, 1998), 29.

[5] Ruth Hayden, *How to Turn Your Money Life Around* (Deerfield Beach, FL: Health Communications, Inc., 1992), 140.

[6] Johnston, Bachman, and O'Malley, *Monitoring the Future,* 166.

[7] Neale S. Godfrey, *A Penny Saved: Teaching Your Children the Values and Life Skills They Will Need to Live in the Real World* (New York: Simon & Schuster, 1995), 17.

### PART 2. CORE MONEY MANAGEMENT ISSUES

[8] Study commissioned by NationsBank and the Consumer Federation of America, February 1997 poll, cited in Stephen C. George, editor, *Money Savvy: How to Live Rich on Any Income* (Emmaus, PA: Rodale Press, 1998), 3.

[9] Janet Bamford, Jeff Blyskal, Emily Card, and Aileen Jacobson, *The Complete Guide to Managing Your Money* (Mount Vernon, NY: Consumers Union, 1989), 119.

[10] Jonathan Pond, *The New Century Family Money Book* (New York: Dell, 1993), 37.

[11] Neal S. Godfrey and Carolina Edwards, *Money Doesn't Grow on Trees: A Parent's Guide to Raising Financially Responsible Children* (New York: Fireside, Simon & Schuster, 1994), 51.

[12] "Can You Say Money Market?" *American Demographics,* February 1988, 22.

[13] Survey conducted by Consumer Federation of America and American Express Travel Related Services Co. Cited in "Teen Survey," *USA Today,* September 12, 1991.

[14] Guinness Media Inc., *The Guinness Book of World Records: 1998,* 280.

[15] Study conducted by Teenage Research Unlimited, cited in Marcia Staimer, "Backing Teen-age Consumers," *USA Today,* February 4, 1992, 1.

[16] Study conducted by Louis Harris and Associates for Liberty Financial Companies in Boston, cited in "Study Sheds New Light on Children's Allowances," *Chicago Tribune,* September 10, 1993.

[17] Stephanie Armour, "Sizzling Computer Skills Replace Flipping Burgers," *USA Today,* April 30, 1999, 1–2.

[18] Ellen Greenberger and Laurence Steinberg, *When Teenagers Work: The Psychological and Social Cost of Adolescent Employment* (New York: Basic Books, 1986), 218-219.

[19] George, editor, *Money Savvy,* 64.

[20] Lewis Mandell, Ph.D., *Our Vulnerable Youth: The Financial Literacy of American 12th Graders* (Washington, DC: Jump$tart Coalition for Personal Financial Literacy, 1998), 68–70.

[21] Quoted in B. J. Towe, "Coming Up With College Funds— Fast!" *Better Homes and Gardens,* October 1994, 36-38.

[22] Pond, *The New Century Family Money Book*, 428-429.

[23] Ibid., 455.

[24] John Waggoner, "Big Funds for Small Investors," *Sesame Street Parents' Guide,* October 1992, 68.

[25] Jane Bryant Quinn, "Clean-Hand Investing," *Newsweek,* May 18, 1992, 57.

[26] This assumes that the investor reinvested all the dividends (money paid quarterly or annually to investors when a company is profitable, which helps raise the price of the stock) and that the stock had a 10.3 percent return on investment (ROI) and the savings account had a 6.8 percent ROI.

[27] Peter Lynch, *Beating the Street* (Simon & Schuster, 1993), cited in "Minnesota Soundbite," *Minnesota Monthly,* May 1993, 13.

[28] Independent Sector, *Volunteering and Giving among Teenagers 12 to 17 Years of Age* (Washington, DC: Independent Sector, 1997), 2-23.

[29] Clint Willis, "Charity Begins at Home," *Family Life,* December 1994/January 1995, 64.

[30] Rick Hampson, "She Gave Up $8.5 Million for Lent," *USA Today,* April 10, 1998, 1-2.

[31] Ibid.

[32] Study conducted by Maritz AmeriPoll, cited in Sandra Block, "How to Be Charitable without Being a Chump," *USA Today,* December 5, 1997, 4.

[33] Andrew Feinberg, "Giving Wisely: How to Choose Charities

That Will Make Your Contributions Count," *Sesame Street Parents' Guide,* December 1993, 50.

[34] Gail Rosenblum, "If I Had a Million," *Minneapolis Star Tribune,* May 3, 1999, E1.

[35] Independent Sector, *Volunteering and Giving among Teenagers 12 to 17 Years of Age*, 1–16, 1–17.

[36] Johnston, Bachman, and O'Malley, *Monitoring the Future*, 199–200.

[37] Independent Sector, *Volunteering and Giving among Teenagers 12 to 17 Years of Age,* 1–18.

[38] Ibid., A-86.

[39] David Elkind, Ph.D., "Going Overboard on Gifts," *Parents,* December 1991, 167.

[40] U.S. Bureau of the Census, "No. 1263: Retail Trade — Establishments, Employees, and Payroll: 1990 and 1994," *Statistical Abstract of the United States: 1997* (117th ed.), Washington, DC: 1997, 766.

[41] Janet L. Fix, "Mall Rats Packing in the Goods," *USA Today*, December 12, 1992, 1.

[42] Margaret Hinchey, *Fund Raisers That Work* (Loveland, CO: Group Books, 1988), 30.

[43] Guinness Media Inc., *The Guinness Book of World Records: 1998*, 296.

[44] "Knock Knock: Should Kids Sell Candy to Strangers?" *Youth Today,* October 1998, 39.

[45] Hinchey, *Fund Raisers That Work,* 18.

[46] Information about the Michigan Community Foundations' Youth Project is listed on the Internet at http://www.mcfyp.org/replic1.html.

[47] Information about the Student Service and Philanthropy Project, which is part of the K-12 Education in Philanthropy Project, is listed on the Web at http://www.msu.edu/~k12phil/sspp.html or is available by contacting the project at 310 West End Avenue, New York, NY 10023-8146; (212) 877-1775.

[48] Robert L. Payton, "The Philanthropic Tradition," in "Youth as Philanthropists: Developing Habits of the Heart" (Fort Wayne, IN: Community Partnerships with Youth, 1999), TFRS 1–5.

[49] Research conducted by Teenage Research Unlimited, cited in Kathleen Stanley, "Teens a Hot Market for Room Accessories," *Minneapolis Star Tribune,* February 27, 1999, 3.

[50] Godfrey and Edwards, *Money Doesn't Grow on Trees,* 59.

[51] George, editor, *Money Savvy,* 56.

[52] Godfrey, *A Penny Saved*, 126.

[53] Research conducted by Teenage Research Unlimited, cited in Stanley, "Teens a Hot Market for Room Accessories," 3.

[54] Joe Dominguez and Vicki Robin, *Your Money or Your Life* (New York: Penguin, 1992), 171.

[55] James Green, Marie Drum Beninati, and Steven Jacober, *Capturing the Purchasing Power of Kids: A Guide to Kids' Interaction at Retail* (Tucson, AZ: Lisa Frank, 1994), 9.

[56] Dan Acuff, Ph.D., *What Kids Buy and Why: The Psychology of Marketing to Kids* (New York: Free Press, 1997), 1.

[57] Green, Beninati, and Jacober, *Capturing the Purchasing Power of Kids,* 22–24.

[58] From a survey of Kids Fashions' First Annual Consumer Survey, December 1993, by BKG. Cited in "Fashion — Kids Take It Personally," *Youth Markets Alert,* March 1994, 4.

[59] "What Kids Buy (and Don't Buy), *Zillions*, January/February 1998, 13

[60] Ibid., 14

[61] "Credit Card Use in the U.S.," study conducted by the University of Michigan Institute for Social Research, cited in Sylvia Porter, *Sylvia Porter's Money Book* (Garden City, NY: Doubleday, 1975), 117.

[62] Ibid., 118.

[63] The answer is six months, and the total interest paid would be $32.30. Although the 15% annual interest rate should technically only come to $15, credit card companies charge 15% on the unpaid portion of your balance each month, making the true interest rate almost double due to paying off the amount in installments.

[64] For example, young people could learn information such as this: Discover has a cash-back bonus award program and does not charge an annual fee. American Express charges an annual fee, and the user must pay off the entire balance each month. Visa and MasterCard charge an annual fee, do not have a cash-back bonus award, and have a minimum payment due each month. The interest rates on Visa and MasterCard vary according to the bank or financial institution they're from.

[65] Guinness Media Inc., *The Guinness Book of World Records: 1998,* 45.

[66] George, editor, *Money Savvy,* 38.

[67] U.S. Bureau of the Census, "No. 781: Percent Distribution of Amount of Debt Held by Families: 1992 and 1995," 513.

[68] Jean Ross Peterson, *It Doesn't Grow on Trees* (White Hall, VA: Betterway Publications, 1988), 35.

[69] Pond, *The New Century Family Money Book*, 384.

[70] George, editor, *Money Savvy,* 124.

[71] Quoted in George, editor, *Money Savvy,* 121.